PRAISE FOR *LIVING CONJURE*

"If you've always dreamt of sitting at the   e
teaches you the ways of folk magic, your wishes have been   r
is a true living encyclopedia of down-home rootwork, and reading *Living Conjure* is like sitting down at the kitchen table with her as she explains the old ways that were handed down to her. If you've been curious about conjure or mystified by magic, this book will gently take you by the hand and give you the tools, rituals, and remedies to take control of your life on your terms."

—MADAME PAMITA, author of *Magical Tarot*, *The Book of Candle Magic*, and Baba *Yaga's Book of Witchcraft*

"Starr Casas is a true occult treasure of the American South, and nothing is more a true practice of the American South than Conjure. The American South's combination of magick—Hoodoo, Christianity, and a peppering of Vodou and American Low Country magickal and spiritual practice—is one of the least understood or discussed. It can be daunting; there is much to understand. Really, when you delve into it, you learn it's largely about good, old-fashioned common sense and getting one's heart and mind synchronized to undertake the art and practice of living a life in which we feel in control and empowered. No one is as nuts, bolts, and most importantly, common sense than Starr. In *Living Conjure*, she brings Conjure out of the shadows and makes it understandable and accessible, and shows the beauty in it that people often don't get to appreciate. She gives examples of lessons in Conjure from her own life—the best way to teach. There is a good dose of humor along with some serious "when to stay in your lane" examples. If the reader doesn't come away from this book with a greater feeling of being grounded and positive, they don't get Conjure. If Starr teaches anything, it is that we can all get and use at least a little Conjure in our lives."

—CLAUDIA WILLIAMS, occult author and owner of Starling Magickal Occult Shop in New Orleans

"Reading *Living Conjure* is like sitting down with Starr Casas and learning at her feet. She gets right into the basics of how to set up your own Conjure practice, making sure you know the why and wherefore of each step. Grab your copy and a cup of tea, and listen to the wisdom of Mama Starr."

—JACKI SMITH, founder of Coventry Creations and author of *Coventry Magic*, *Do It Yourself Akashic Wisdom*, and *The Big Book of Candle Magic*

"*Living Conjure: The Practice of Southern Folk Magic* by Starr Casas is a captivating exploration of Southern folk magic. Casas masterfully brings the magic of the South to life, sharing her deep knowledge and personal experiences with an inviting and engaging style. The book delves into setting up an altar, interpreting signs and omens such as the symbolism in animals and numbers, and offers a wealth of recipes that are sure to help you through difficult times. Each charm and spell is explained clearly and thoroughly, providing a genuine perspective from someone who has grown up with and practiced these traditions. This book is a fantastic resource for anyone interested in Southern Conjure or folk magic. Casas's expertise and deep connection to this mystical world shine through every page, making it both informative and enchanting. Starr Casas does it again, delivering another masterpiece of Southern folk magic."

>   —MYSTIC DYLAN, author of *Throwing Bones, Crystals, Stones, and Curios*

"*Living Conjure* is a wonderful introduction to Conjure. Author Starr Casas wrote this book in the way she teaches. As I read it, I felt like I was back in The Conjure Academy, listening to her lessons. Starr explains the significance of the foundations of Conjure; for example, the importance of the Bible and honoring ancestors. Starr also explains how to figure out which passages are most relevant for your specific magical work. This book provides everything you need to know to start practicing effective Conjure works. I wish I had it when I began my journey with Conjure several years ago."

>   —CHARITY BEDELL, author of *Container Magic* and coauthor of *The Good Witches Guide: A Modern-Day Wiccapedia of Magickal Ingredients and Spells*

"It's been said before that Starr Casas is a national treasure—and this certainly bears repeating! The Queen of Conjure has given her growing legion of readers another gem of a book that is as powerful as it is practical and as mystical as it is masterful! Seasoned practitioners will rejoice at the wealth of information in these pages, and new seekers will quickly realize that they are beginning their spiritual journeys with the lessons of a supremely gifted and knowledgeable teacher. Whether you want to know more about how to set up an altar, use prayers and offerings, or understand the subtle signs and symbols hidden in nature, Casas has you covered. *Living Conjure* is a must-read for anyone eager to live a magical life."

>   —ANTONIO PAGLIARULO, author of *The Evil Eye: The History, Mystery*, and *Magic of the Quiet Curse*

LIVING
CONJURE

LIVING CONJURE

The Practice of Southern Folk Magic

STARR CASAS

Foreword by Jake Richards

WEISER BOOKS

This edition first published in 2024 by Weiser Books, an imprint of
Red Wheel/Weiser, LLC
with offices at:
65 Parker Street, Suite 7
Newburyport, MA 01950
www.redwheelweiser.com

ISBN: 978-1-57863-824-6
Library of Congress Cataloging-in-Publication Data
Names: Casas, Starr, author. | Richards, Jake, 1997- writer of foreword.
Title: Living conjure : the practice of Southern folk magic / Starr Casas ;
    foreword by Jake Richards.
Other titles: Practice of Southern folk magic
Description: Newburyport, MA : Weiser Books, 2024. | Summary: "This is a
    beginner's guide to Conjure written by an authentic Conjure woman with
    over four decades of working experience. The author learned Conjure the
    old-fashioned way: at home, from her relatives and ancestors. She leads
    readers step by step toward establishing their own practice, from
    setting up altars to finding the right tools to creating baths, washes,
    and powders, as well as introducing readers to the culture and customs
    that brought these workings to light"—Provided by publisher.
Identifiers: LCCN 2024012658 | ISBN 9781578638246 (trade paperback) | ISBN
    9781633413252 (ebook)
Subjects: LCSH: Hoodoo (Cult) | Magic--Southern States. |
    Folklore—Southern States. | BISAC: BODY, MIND & SPIRIT / Magick Studies
    | SOCIAL SCIENCE / Folklore & Mythology
Classification: LCC BL2490 .C37 2024 | DDC 133.4/30975--dc23/
eng/20240402
LC record available at https://lccn.loc.gov/2024012658

Cover design by Sky Peck Design
Cover illustrations by Creative Market/Annie Konst
Interior by Maureen Forys, Happenstance Type-O-Rama
Typeset in Macklin Slab and Intro

Printed in the United States of America
IBI
10 9 8 7 6 5 4 3 2 1

*I dedicate this book to all my elders,
and all those ancestors who came before me.*

CONTENTS

PART IV:
Tools of the Trade

PART V:
Make It Yourself—
Oils, Washes, Powders, and Candles

EVEN SNAKES HOLD WISDOM

One day, a lil girl was walking down a dirt road. On the side of the road was a large rock, and upon the rock was a very large snake sunning itself in the sun. Now the lil girl wasn't afraid because she knew that even a snake holds some wisdom. When she got closer and the snake saw her, the snake said, "Hello, missy."

She said, "Good day to you, snake."

Snake said, "How are you this fine day?"

She politely said, "I am wonderful today. How are you?"

Snake says, "Oh, I am having a great day on this warm rock."

She said, "Well, you be blessed. I gotta be getting home."

Snake said, "Why don't you come and enjoy the sun with me on this fine day?"

She knew that even though the snake held wisdom, he could also be real tricky, and if she got real close he would strike. So she said, "Oh no, sir, I can't today as I have to return home but maybe another day."

The snake hissed and said, "Okay missy, I'll be here. You can come visit anytime!"

The lil girl skipped all the way home knowing that the wisdom her mama had given her had kept her safe another day! Just because someone might act cool doesn't mean they have your best interest at heart. Like the lil girl, you can be nice to them but keep them at arms' length and take what they say with a grain of salt. All folks have wisdom, just some's is a lil saltier than others.

Be mindful. Conjure on!

FOREWORD

"Use it up, wear it out; make do or do without."

This was an often-echoed order and teaching for many children who grew up in the South. As children, we'd often roll our eyes at it—secretly of course, less we get back handed! But we often don't understand the underlying meanings this saying has, from the experiences of those who recite it, until we get older. It has the same feel and is along the same meaning as the saying there is "a time and a season for everything," which folks get from Ecclesiastes 3:1-8:

To every thing there is a season, and a time to every purpose under the heaven:

A time to be born, and a time to die; a time to plant, and a time to pluck up that which is planted;

A time to kill, and a time to heal; a time to break down, and a time to build up;

A time to weep, and a time to laugh; a time to mourn, and a time to dance;

A time to cast away stones, and a time to gather stones together; a time to embrace, and a time to refrain from embracing;

A time to get, and a time to lose; a time to keep, and a time to cast away;

A time to rend, and a time to sew; a time to keep silence, and a time to speak;

A time to love, and a time to hate; a time of war, and a time of peace.

Upon hearing these for the first time, they hold just about the same weight for the young Southern child as the favored saying of the home every time the child doesn't want to eat whatever's been made for supper—"Use it up, wear it out; make do or do without." But, like that saying, these verses begin to hold more weight and take a better shape over time as we go through life, learning everything it talks about. Knowing when to keep giving, and when to know enough is enough. Knowing when to go to war or not. Knowing when to laugh or cry. Knowing what to keep or toss out, as we shed the many selves we are always becoming as we grow and go through life. This verse is also the basis for the old folks' steadfast belief and following of the famed *Farmer's Almanac* when planting their crops, or cutting their hair, quitting bad habits, weaning a baby, or even having a tooth pulled. "Don't forget your roots" is another favored saying of my own mama, to always remind me to renew where I come from.

I was born and raised in the mountains of East Tennessee, spending much of my childhood traipsing through these hills and woods, whether in Tennessee, North Carolina, or Virginia. While adding to the horror and shock of my mother when I waltzed right up to and under a bull in a field or when I picked up a copperhead Daddy caught in the minnow trap. I was a hellion, is what I'm saying.

I am an Appalachian Conjure man and faith healer, after those of my own blood and bones. I've been doing this for well over a decade now but using the word "doing" don't feel right. I've lived with it and been exposed to it all my life. From fishing trips where we left tobacco on the bank, helping fill the money jug by the door with found money; to helping Mama wash the walls and always making sure there was at least one light on in the house at all times. No matter if it's Appalachia, the Ozarks, the Low Country, or the Deep South, these traditions are lived. They are as second nature to us, as is the tying of our shoes or the way we sweep a broom or how we put on pants.

Since I can first remember, I was fed stories of haints and spirits, of people I never met knowing all about me and always watching over me, and of stories of some of those people dealing with witches who turned into cats or into hogs. Growing up, I stepped over salt lines when leaving the house to go to school and slept in my bed over bowls of ice water, lathered with Vicks VapoRub, and the taste of onion juice still on my tongue when I was sick. I never asked why, it's just what we did. It was normal. It's what we had always done, and it worked, so why question it? Just like it was normal watching Papaw preach and cast spirits off people or stop the flowing of blood when he said the right Bible verse. Or when he anointed my sister, born premature, at birth. There was a bruise left where he anointed her on the forehead, but after that she progressed just fine, as well as any healthy child would.

My ears became able to discern the difference between the yowl or scream of a bobcat or panther and that of the banshee, who came to foretell a death. My ears also learned to tell when the Ghost had gotten on Papaw: he'd start getting the jumping breath in his preaching voice before the hooping and hollering started. The first things my hands caught weren't hearts or money, but rather fish and fireflies. My taste was crafted through homemade apple butter and baked onion juice when we were sick. We hear it, feel it, taste it, smell it, and live it.

I wasn't raised ignorant or "backward." Most here weren't, until we grew up and the world told us we had been. "Don't forget your roots." That's when you have to remember, folks like that weren't there, weren't raised here, and they weren't reared on the spirits of the dead in the cemetery or the Spirit when it comes down on the preacher man. They weren't brought up in the struggle of "low" folks, but still expect us to "catch up" to the rest of the nation and the world in just about every aspect of life. Except what catching up do we have to do, with Southern culture that has not only preserved in flesh and blood this nation's history, and the roots of many people, but has also preserved things from before the birth of this nation. When I speak of Southern culture, I am not referring to Confederate flags or any bigotry like that. That ain't Southern culture.

Southern culture is NASCAR originating through hillbillies and rednecks rigging their cars to outrun the law. Southern culture is waging a battle against the Big Man and the mining companies during the Coal Wars. Southern culture is the revolution and freedom of Black Americans. Southern culture is making do or doing without, in every aspect of life. It's knowing when to fight or back down. When to love or hate and where to put your trust and loyalty. "Don't forget your roots."

That's what I take from my mama's words. Don't forget where you come from, what stock you're made of, and what has been done to get your ass here neither. Don't go walking off in life trying to leave behind the path that's been cleared for you by generations of blood and sweat, of weeping and laughing. Don't go walking on the land without recognizing the soil that's been tilled and sowed to feed generations for you to be here.

That's why trees don't walk. If they could, they'd have to leave behind those big roots they spent so long running and mapping deep into the earth. Your ancestors and culture and heritage don't begin or end with you. But you owe it to those before you to act like you're something. Not more than or less than. *Something.* Not something like them over there or down the road. Something like you. Something like the only you that could've come from their strength and struggles. And if you leave it behind, you're walking away from a deep tap root that has been generations in the making, splitting time and space and bridging the past and present to guide and help you.

The roots guide the plant, like hands fumbling around in the dark. The first ones to fumble struggle to find water. But the new roots that come, their struggle isn't as hard, because they sprout from the roots that already grew to get to some water; they've already mapped out the best spots for absorbing moisture. And soon, roots sprout and they end up surrounded by everything they will ever need. But if something happens, they know exactly what to do.

In the following conversation—I won't call it a work or a book, because it reads just like she's talking to you, all of her writing does, 'cause she is—but when you talk to Mama Starr, she's gonna get it through your head that to do this work you need the spirit of discernment, you need "eyes to see, and ears to hear." You can't just jump in. There's generations-worth of understanding behind it. The verses I gave before are exactly for that, knowing when the right time for something is. When it's best to lose something or gain something, for battle or peace. As I always say, an ounce of precaution is worth more than a pound of cure or, in some cases, whoop-ass!

Mama Starr has laid her practices out in such a way that you as the reader can best get your footing in this, or even recognize some things from your own childhood. As an author along the same lines myself, I know the sacrifice it takes to give information like this. Information that feels a part of you and where you come from. Remember that as you go on. Writing a book ain't easy, and neither is giving what feels like a part of yourself away for the sake of its survival.

In the pages that follow are the foundations of a Southern folk magic tradition that grew out of struggles and revolution. It grew out of making do with what you got. While Starr's way of doing things is different from mine, us being from different parts of the South, the prevailing spirit of resilience, resistance, and independence is still there, waiting in the outstretched palms of hands from generations before.

Before you can even try to forget your roots, you must find them. I think everyone can learn something here, whether this is a tradition you grew up with or you simply find wisdom you can apply to your own. And maybe soon, you'll be anointing your life with this work and dusting the steps you take to achieve every good thing your ancestors hoped and wished for you. "Don't forget your roots."

I won't keep you though. It's a long road and a long life ahead. Remember: discernment. In everything. And may you be as honest with the spirits who walk with you, as you are able to be honest with yourself.

May your roots run deep.
Jake "Dr. Buck" Richards

ACKNOWLEDGMENTS

I'd like to acknowledge my mama, who taught me how important my culture and my ancestors are. She also taught me that I can do anything I set my mind to and the only person who can stop me is me! Also, my fourth-grade teacher, Mrs. Hall. I can close my eyes and see her with all her rings and bracelets on, the long flowing skits; and her hair was always pulled up in a bun on top of her head. She taught us so much that year about flowers, and now I know she was teaching us magic, how to listen to what the outside is saying. I think it was the first time I ever came in contact with a witch, and I loved her. She taught us to make candles with Gulf wax and to color them with broken crayons that she kept in a box, and how to press flowers, and how to crochet. The stories she would tell us at story time. She is long gone now, but she will always live on in my heart.

LIVING CONJURE

INTRODUCTION

This is the first book of this kind that I have written. Not the first Conjure book, but the first book that I have really tried to write for folks of all experience levels: from those who don't know anything about Conjure to those who know a lot about Conjure. One of my students, Miss Deb, asked me to write this book. Miss Deb has been with me for probably about twelve years now; she suggested that I write this book because she felt like my other books do not necessarily fit the beginner. This book was kind of hard for me to write—not because I don't have the knowledge to write it, but because I did not learn from a book.

I learned what I know over years. I learned through stories and interacting with my elders. Nobody sat me down like I was in school and said, "Look, you're gonna learn this, this, this, this, and this today." It wasn't like that. I did not learn through the written word; I learned through stories and lessons and by example. So, when Miss Deb asked me to write this book, I didn't have a clue where to start because I've never learned one thing at the time in order. So setting this book up was really kind of tricky because I had to try to think the way someone who is new to Conjure would think, to think about what it is that you need to know in order to have a strong foundation within this work.

When I teach hands-on classes or take on a student, they are taught the way that I was taught: through actions through stories and, yes, through lessons. Writing a book that teaches someone who has never done this work before, sitting down and trying to piece it all together, has been a little tricky for me because I don't even know, or I should say I don't remember, when I learned the first thing about Conjure. It's been in my life since I was a child. I didn't want to just write a beginner's book; What I wanted to write was a book that would help folks, from someone who doesn't know anything about the work to someone who's been working for a while.

The information in this book is important and needs to be written down, because a lot of the elders are passing on. If this information isn't shared, then it will just be gone. There will not be anymore. One problem is new generations have lost respect for their elders, and so the elders have stepped back away from them. In this work, honor and respect are a big deal. I was raised to believe that if you don't respect your elders and the folks around you, then you truly have no respect for yourself. If you are going to do this work, then being respectful needs to be at the top of your list. Respect is a must to have a strong foundation within this work: you have to remember that to get respect, you've got to give respect. If you are one of those folks who is very disrespectful, then how can you expect the spirits to work with you if you don't show them respect?

In writing this book, I've tried to think how my children and my grandchildren and even my great-grandchildren learn about the work. This brought my great-granddaughter Queenie to mind. From the moment she was able to crawl around, she would always go straight for the candles. I pour my own candles, and I had poured the orange candle that I planned on doing work with; it was on the lower shelf in my office and she found it. She would always go to that same candle and hold it and roll it around and just look at it. I guess she liked the way the candle felt or the energies that were coming off of the candle from the prayers that were prayed into the candle when I poured. Every time we would try to take that candle away from her, she would start crying so I told my granddaughter just to let her play with it as long as she didn't put it in her mouth. What started as a fascination with candles then turned into a fascination with my altars.

One day my daughter and my granddaughter and Queenie were in the kitchen just hanging out. I don't even know when Queenie ended up in the living room at my ancestor altar, but she had went to the altar and she was just standing there looking around and talking her baby talk to the altar. She was around two or two-and-a-half years old at that time; she's now seven. From that time on, she knew that those were her people on the altar, that that was her blood. I truly believe that the ancestors called her to that altar and that they enjoyed her standing there talking to them in words that only she could understand. I suppose they understood what she was saying, too. It's not that we talked to her about the ancestors; she went up to the altar on her own and it was just explained to her. This is the way my kids and my grandkids were taught, just like I was taught. I have never sat down with them and said, "If you have this situation, you do this. If you need this, you do this. If something is going on, do this." That's not how they learned. They learned by watching me work and listening to me and coming to me when they need help with something that is going on in their lives.

You know, when I was growing up, there was an old tale about the plat eye. If we didn't tell the truth, my mama would tell us you are lying like a plat eye. The plat eye is a monster with red eyes, and the more you lie, the bigger the monster gets. This is an old tale, I'm sure, from before my mama's childhood. It's a tale used to teach honesty. She never said that the monster was going to get us; she simply pointed out that every time you tell a lie, you have to tell another one and another one and another one until the lie is as big as the plat eye. There are a lot of tales that are told that pertain to this work, like Brer Rabbit, who you will meet later on in this book. The work is literally hidden within these tales. The ancestors of this work learned to hide the work in plain sight—that is why this work is called tricks.

It is my goal to write in an understanding and understandable way, so that even the novice will be able to pick up the work and build a strong foundation. Even though these works may seem simple, they are very powerful, and they shouldn't be played with, not ever. Just because these works seem simple and easy does not mean that they can't truly cause harm. I repeat this in every book that I write because it's important: we should always remember that every action causes a reaction, and we are responsible for all the works that we do. Also, just because you know something, and know how to do something, doesn't mean that you can jump in with both feet and just do whatever you want to do. You have to take responsibility for every job you do within this work. It's not a free-for-all; never has been, never will be.

Those who've read my books and are familiar with my writings will see some of the things in the beginner's section that are similar to previous things I've already written. One time I had somebody contact me and say, "Starr, why did you write about that type of work? Even though it was different, it was along the same lines as things that you wrote about in the past." I explained to them, because someone new may be reading my book for the first time and they won't have a clue what in the world I'm talking about. I have come to the conclusion that whenever I'm writing, I cannot assume that the reader knows or understands the work. There is always someone new. That's why I'm writing this book. I try to never repeat the same work in a book, but you have to understand that there are a lot of ways to do a job. The works are all going to start with prayer. They are all going to start with some type of setup; they are all going to start with some type of roots, herbs, oils, powders—and even though they achieve the same goal, they're going to be worked different. I want this book to be something that everyone, from the novice to the experienced worker, can gain some knowledge from. With every book I write, I do so for the ancestors of this work to show homage to them and honor to them.

I hope that you find some useful works and information within these pages. The information is meant to help you build a strong foundation within this work. I am by no means the begin all and end all of Conjure. I am simply trying to share as much information as I can, because I am getting up in age and with the age comes forgetfulness. This work is too important to be lost, and the ancestors are too important to be forgotten!

Questions and Answers

These are a few basic questions that come up a lot for new Conjure students.

WHAT IS A PETITION?

A petition is basically what you would like to have happen.
For example, a short petition could be as simple as "I petition the spirits that walk with me to get the blue car with tag XXXXXX."

WHAT IS A PERSONAL PRAYER?

A personal prayer is a private prayer that you pray when you need help. It is not a written prayer from the Bible or a book; it is a prayer that comes from your heart straight to spirit.

WHAT IS A NOVENA?

A novena is a prayer that is said over a certain number of days, like the nine-day novena to St. Martha.

WHAT ARE ROOTS AND HERBS?

Roots and herbs are used in a work for extra power or to pull the spirit of the plant or root into the work.

WHAT ARE CONJURE OILS?

Conjure oils—or condition oils, as some folks call them—are spiritual oils that are made with ingredients and prayers. They are added to candles, Conjure bags, and other spiritual works to bring about the results you are looking for.

WHAT ARE SPIRITUAL BATHS?

Spiritual baths, or what some call spiritual washes, are made of roots, herbs, and sometimes spiritual waters—it all depends on what the bath is for. Spiritual baths are added to your bathwater and are worked with for many different types of conditions. Usually baths are taken in sets of three, five, or seven days. Either before or after the bath, some do prayers, candles, and/or meditation.

WHAT ARE CONJURE POWDERS?

Conjure powders are made from herbs, roots, dirts from different (oftentimes powerful) places, and other items. Conjure powders are worked with to bring about a change of some kind. You can lay tricks with them, you can roll candles in them, you can wear them, or you can powder items with them. They are worked with for dressing or wearing too. Most powders are made from herbs, roots, and dirt from powerful places.

WHO ARE THE ANCESTORS OF CONJURE?

The ancestors of Conjure are the folks who were brought over here during the time of slavery. They brought with them the knowledge of what we now call Conjure, Hoodoo, or Root-work. Conjure, Hoodoo, and Rootwork are all the same thing. When I was growing up, I never heard Hoodoo being used as the name for this work. Hoodoo was a question: "Hoodoo you?" Meaning, "Who put roots on you?" In the time of the internet, it has become one of the names for this work.

PART I

The Foundation of Conjure

When I speak of the ancestors, I am speaking of those who brought this work here through their suffering in the times of slavery. If it were not for them, Conjure wouldn't be here. Conjure was born out of slavery, from folks trying to survive during a time when white folks felt they had the right to own another person like they were cattle. They are the foundation of this work; it is their knowledge from their homeland intertwined with Christianity that brought Conjure to life. Christianity was already on the continent of Africa during the times of the slave trade. It is possible that some people on the continent had already become Christian before coming to America. This does not mean that I personally believe that the enslaved ancestors were already Christian when they were stolen from their homeland—I do, however, believe that Christianity was known in Africa before slavery.

We need to understand that not all of the people that were kidnapped were from the same area. They didn't all speak the same language and so therefore we should understand that they had different customs that they practiced in their homelands. But when they were brought over here on the slave ships, they were just all put together. I'm no scholar, but I believe—and my common sense tells me—that Conjure is built from different areas of Africa. When the ancestors were brought to the South to be sold and to be placed on plantations, each area of the South had their own customs. It's not like it's all the same, just like each area of Africa has its own distinct differences. Conjure work varies from place to place, because the customs of the people in the South vary from place to place. I believe that may be because the first and second generation of the ancestors who were bought over here into slavery tried to keep their customs from their homeland. But as we see today with our young people, customs get watered down. You also have to take into effect what the slave owner would allow and what they wouldn't allow.

The plantation owners feared the ancestors. The ancestors were not allowed to play drums or get together in large groups—it was forbidden. As a matter of fact, there was a law passed that said the ancestors could not congregate in large groups. If the churches of today are any example of what the churches were like back then, I'm sure that they looked at the ancestors as heathens. They took it upon themselves to force the ancestors to become Christian. They didn't realize that they were giving them the tools they needed to practice their religion. They weren't allowed to have drums, so they clapped their hands and stomped their feet to the rhythm of the music in church. Going to the prayer house was really the only way that they could all gather without being watched. I would think that is the day when the plantation owners relaxed and didn't really worry about what they were doing. It was assumed that they were praying and worshipping God. I know from growing up with my mama that speaking in riddles was a way that messages could be shared without the plantation owners realizing what was happening; and the prayer house was the perfect place for it. While the preacher was preaching the sermon, it is possible that he was also sending a hidden message to the people.

The ancestors were not given credit for their intelligence. While some of them were taught to read, the majority of them were not. The plantation owners underestimated them, and it worked in their favor. I can understand that this helped them. They were allowed to have the Bible, which they turned to work for them. The Old Testament is full of Conjure work.

One of the figures in the Bible who has a strong foundation in Conjure work is Moses. Mother Harriet Tubman took on the name Mama Moses when she was bringing the ancestors out of slavery into freedom. Elders teach and understand how powerful the Old Testament can be. Since the ancestors were forced to become Christian, they put the Bible to good use. Moses is important because of the things that he achieved in the Bible; but not only that, the Bible tells us that Moses was able to speak directly to God. The Bible also tells us that Moses is the only human who was ever allowed to see God. He wanted to see God, he wanted to look at Him, so God placed him in the crevice of a big old rock and passed by him, and the Bible says that Moses saw God's back. Conjure workers believe that to be true, so it had to be passed down through the generations.

God favored Moses when He sent him against the magicians of Pharaoh because Pharaoh had challenged God's word. Moses was sent to set the people free, and when Pharaoh's magicians conjured up snakes, Moses threw his staff down and it turned into a snake and it ate the snakes that the magicians had conjured. Through the generations of the ancestors sharing the information about this work, Moses, like the other prophets, are a big part of this work.

I know it's hard for some folks to accept the fact that Christianity was forced on the ancestors, and that it is a big part of this work through the Bible, but it is also part of the ancestors even though they were forced into Christianity. You can't throw the baby out with the bathwater; if you do, you are weakening the foundation that the ancestors built through their blood, sweat, and tears. The Bible is a powerful book. Churches are man-made, they're run by men and set the rules. The Bible is a book of wisdom, and it has some powerful information in it. Also, whether we like it or not, the Bible is part of the foundation of Conjure work.

There is more to the foundation of this work than the magical side—that is just one side of it. The foundation also extends to the food, the language, the churches, and also the way that you live everyday life. It is the whole culture, not just a piece of it. It's more than the magic of Conjure; it's the whole way of life.

The best example that I can show you is the Gullah Geechee people. They are the descendants of Africans who were brought over here to Sea Island and Atlantic coastal plantations. They have their own language which came about because the ancestors did not all come from the same place. The Gullah people have kept up with the traditions of the ancestors when it comes to food, music, arts, and crafts. They are as close to the ancestors as you are going to get, and they were raised in Christianity.

The thing we really need to look at is that there is mainstream Christianity, and then there is the Christianity of the Conjure worker, the ancestors—they are definitely two different types of churches. The churches of white folks are completely different from the churches that the ancestors built, even though they are both Christian places.

The Gullah people have kept up with the customs and the culture of the ancestors. Today, a lot of their lands and traditions are being lost to outsiders. It is really sad and hurtful to see a culture and its traditions being destroyed by the outside. The Gullah people are the true descendants, and if you really want to understand the customs and culture of this work, that is the place to start. They are the foundation that this work sets on. I would advise you to go visit some of the sea islands where the

Gullah have restaurants and shops that sell grass baskets and other items that they learned to make from one generation to the next.

For me, the customs that I grew up with just happened to intertwine with this work. It's all I know. For me, it's a way of life. It's how I live, it's how I raised my children, and it's how my grandchildren have been raised. It's all I know. And I feel like the ancestors should be honored and uplifted and never forgotten because they are the foundation that this work is built on. I feel like that should be one of the most important parts of this work. When I say my personal prayers daily, I always say a prayer for the ancestors who came before me, for the ancestors who suffered, for the ancestors who were maimed, murdered, and killed, because without them there would be no Conjure.

The best way to understand this work and to gather the knowledge that you need to be a successful worker is to understand the culture and the people that all work comes from. This work was never meant to be out in the world. Until the internet, it was only passed down through families and taught by elders. Now it is everywhere, but the foundation of the work is missing; because the foundation of this work is the ancestors, the culture, and the customs, it is not now, nor has it ever been, just about the work. There are dark works within Conjure, but the main focus of the work is healing and taking care of the family. That is being lost in today's materialistic world. The respect for the ancestors of this work is almost nonexistent in today's world, but it should be one of the most important things about this work because they are the foundation of this work and they should be remembered and held up high.

1

Folk Tales and Ole Spirituals

The ancestors were very good at hiding information in the old spirituals and children's tales. I grew up on Brer Rabbit. I was being taught Conjure without being told what it was. As far as I knew, these were just stories that had lessons in them. We need to get back to telling stories to our children. You can talk to them all day and they might remember some of it, but if you tell them a good tale, they will remember it.

Brer Rabbit and the Tar Baby

Some of my favorite stories were those with Brer Rabbit, a trickster who always managed to best Brer Fox. Many of these stories incorporate pieces of Conjure. This retelling of *Brer Rabbit and the Tar Baby* is my own.

> *Brer Fox hated Brer Rabbit. Brer Rabbit played tricks, he was always bossin' other folks around, and Brer Fox hated it. He decided that he was gonna kill Brer Rabbit if it was the last thing that he ever did! He thought about how he could get rid of that Brer Rabbit once and for all, and he came up with a plan: he was going to make a tar baby. He got some coal tar and some turpentine and mixed them*

*together and made a baby out of them. He put a hat on his
tar baby and put her in the middle of the road where he
knew Brer Rabbit would find her. Then he hid and waited.*

When I was young, tar water wash was used for cleansing and protection. Turpentine is also worked with for cleansing and protection. My mama used to mark our shoes with it, and we were given a drop or two on a tablespoon of sugar once a year to kill any "live things" in us we might have. Also, tar sticks, and once it hardens you're not going to be able to remove it.

Shoes under the bed are a big thing in old style Conjure works. The works are done to nail the target down and keep their behind at home. Back in the day, this work was done on men who couldn't keep their behinds at home and were out tomcatting all night. You never threw away an old pair of shoes because an enemy could get them and use them against you; they were always burned. Most folks only had two pair of shoes, so to do the trick on the target you would have to wait to get the shoes. Once you got the shoes, you put tar on each sole and placed them under their side of the bed, one shoe in front of the other, like they were walking under the bed. Once the tar dried, the shoes were stuck under there and the target should be stuck at home in his bed and not someone else's bed.

Rude is something southern children are taught never to be from a very young age. You are to always be polite to folks. So as the story goes, when Brer Rabbit came along the road and inquired as to the tar baby's day, and the tar baby didn't answer Brer Rabbit after he spoke several times, he became furious at her rudeness and attacked, just as Brer Fox knew he would! But because the tar baby was made of sticky tar, all that Brer Rabbit accomplished was getting his paw stuck. The lesson here is to think before you act! Make sure you look at the whole picture, and never let your temper get the best of you like Brer Rabbit did. Always keep a cool head. My mama used these tales as learning tools to show us what not to do and what can happen if you go jumping in with both feet without thinking.

*"Lemme go! Lemme go or I'll hit you again!" Brer Rabbit
yelled.*

The Tar Baby said nothing.

*Brer Rabbit took a swing at the Tar Baby with his other
paw, and of course it got stuck in the sticky coal tar. Both
his paws were stuck! Still hidden in the bushes out of sight,
Brer Fox danced with glee. His plan was working!*

Because Brer Rabbit lost his temper and didn't think before he
acted, he not only got one paw stuck, he now has both of his paws stuck.
This could have been avoided had he thought instead of acted when the
first paw got stuck. My mama used to tell us "a hard head makes a soft
behind," meaning every action causes a reaction, and if you continue to
not listen, then it is going to be a hard lesson coming that you will never
forget. Brer Rabbit has a hard lesson to learn about that temper of his
and controlling it instead of letting it control him.

*Brer Rabbit decided that he was going to kick the tar out of
the Tar Baby. He sprang at her with both feet, and his feet
sank into the Tar Baby's sticky little body.*

*Brer Rabbit was furious! Both his paws were stuck and now
so were both his feet. He headbutted the Tar Baby but that
just ended up with him covered with tar and stuck to the
spot. He couldn't move an inch.*

Once again, Brer Rabbit's temper has gotten him in a mess—exactly
what Brer Fox wanted to have happen. Sometimes our enemies will
poke and prod us to make us act out of character, just like ole Brer Fox
played Brer Rabbit. Always try to keep a cool head, and don't act out in
a temper, lest you end up like Brer Rabbit and your enemy has a good
laugh at your expense. These are important lessons if you are going to
be a good Conjure worker.

*It was time for Brer Fox to make himself known. He strolled
out of the bushes and up to Brer Rabbit.*

"Well, well, well," he gloated. "What have we here?"

And he grinned real wide.

*Brer Rabbit swallowed hard. He had to think fast while
Brer Fox was busy rolling on the ground and laughing
about how he was stuck.*

Now Brer Rabbit sees what he didn't see before his enemy had him right where he wanted him. Brer Fox had laid the trick and he fell for it because he acted without thinking. Now the tables are turned, though, because Brer Fox is too busy gloating and doesn't realize that now that Brer Rabbit knows what is going on, he has a plan. Plant the seed and the tree will grow. Brer Rabbit is on it now!

> *"Oh, Brer Fox! You can drown me, hang me, roast me over an open fire," pleaded Brer Babbit. "But please, please, Brer Fox! Don't throw me into the briar patch!"*

Brer Fox did exactly what Brer Rabbit wanted. He slung him into the briar patch, not realizing that briars are very protective. He listened and heard nothing until Brer Rabbit called his name and said,

> *"I was born and bred in the briar patch," Brer Rabbit said. "Born and bred in the briar patch."*
>
> *He skipped away along the road as Brer Fox gnashed his teeth in anger.*

Sometimes we get too full of ourselves, like Brer Rabbit, and we play right into our enemy's hands! Never work when you are angry because you can't think straight. This is a good lesson for all of us to remember. Don't let your emotions get you played by an enemy like ole Brer Rabbit did!

Just like the tale of Brer Rabbit and Brer Fox, there are many tales and works in the Bible that are being lost because elders or either dying off without teaching them or they don't have anyone to share them with. Either way, this important information is being lost and forgotten. Once it is lost, there is no getting it back. This is why I write books—to share what I can share before it is all gone.

Ole Spirituals

Back in the day of the elders, the old spirituals were more than just Christian tunes. They were a way to get messages from one place to the next without the slave owner knowing what was going on. The owners of these plantations underestimated the folks that they had chained to the plantations. The elders outsmarted them at every turn. Like the Brer Rabbit tales, these old spirituals hold secrets.

A lot of folks in today's world who do this type of work don't know about the secrets that are hidden within the old spirituals. This work is called tricks for reason—back in the time of slavery, the ancestors had to be tricky. They had to learn to work around the plantation owners. I'm not going to go into great detail about the old spirituals, but I did want to share some with you so you know what to look for so you can kind of understand how the work works. The ancestors of this work were highly intelligent. They learned how to maneuver around the master to get things done and help their families and the families of their community.

I have noticed that in today's world of Conjure, due to folks being anti-church and anti-Christian, they have tried to take the Bible out of Conjure. I never try to convince anybody of anything. Folks can do whatever they want to do—that's their business. I'm not going to get into any big debates or anything over the Bible in Conjure. That's not my place. But what I will do in my writings is show how the Bible plays a part in this work. Then it's up to the reader to decide for themselves.

In the times of slavery, there were no doctors for the slaves on the plantation. The slave owners didn't provide for their health or well-being—they were lucky if they had food to eat. Each plantation had its own healers who took care of everybody. Some called them doctors, some called them root women and root men. They were the ones who took care of the people. They were the healers.

"There Is a Balm in Gilead"

Here's an example of not only how these healers could get a message out about someone being sick but also the importance of the Bible in that time. If you look at Jeremiah 8:22, you will see that it talks about balm of Gilead:

> *Is there no balm in Gilead,*
> *Is there no physician there?*
> *Why then is there no recovery*
> *For the health of the daughter of my people?*

Within that verse they are asking, "Is there no doctor? And will there be no recovery?"

Now let's take a look at a spiritual mentioning balm of Gilead. This old spiritual dates back to sometime in the nineteenth century. The balm of Gilead is worked with in peaceful home work. It can be worked with to bring peace to a marriage. You could also work with it to bring peace between friends. It is one of those herbs that is worked with to soothe.

"Balm in Gilead"

There is a balm in Gilead
To make the wounded whole
There is a balm in Gilead
To heal the sin-sick soul

In this section, if we look at it, we understand that someone is in deep pain. Something is going on with them, they're very ill. Now, if we look at the word *balm*, it means "to soothe," so if I heard someone singing this song, I would assume that medication was needed to help the person who is ill to get well. Because there were no doctors for the ancestors held in slavery, many times they passed away due to illness, being beaten to death, or just out and out killed.

Let's look at another stanza. This could be taken two different ways, and we're going to look at both of them.

If you cannot preach like Peter,
if you cannot be like Paul,
you can tell the love of Jesus
and say, "He died to save us all."

If you know your Bible and you know the story of St. Peter, St. Peter was a leader. He was well trusted and he believed in what he was doing. So when I look at that: if you can't pray like Peter and if you can't be like Paul then you need to go tell someone who has that power within them to help. A strong healer is needed to help with this illness that is going on—that's one way to look at that and the other way would mean that the person who was ill has passed. But if you really look at that and look at that very last stanza, it says he died to save us all. Is it possible that maybe this elder tried to escape and got caught, and maybe he got beat near half to death, but he never told on anyone else. So therefore he was strong like Peter, he believed like Paul, and he kept his mouth shut so no one else was harmed. Look at those words: he saved us all.

A lot of these secrets are being lost because the elders are passing on. Folks are learning online now. Sometimes folks get upset with me because I share so much. I share it because if I don't, when I'm gone what's in my head is going to be gone. This work has to live on, and writing about it and teaching about it is the only way I know how to do my part. I want to look at one more spiritual just so you get the idea of how to understand what is hidden and what it means to this work.

"Follow the Drinking Gourd"

The next old spiritual we're going to look at is "Follow the Drinking Gourd." In this spiritual, the stanzas actually give you directions. I want to say this: you know, it amazes me, the arrogance of the slave owners, and also their stupidity. I guess no matter what century you live in, assumptions still run wild. They captured these people, brought them over here in chains. They assumed that they weren't intelligent, that they were lower than animals, and yet they were the ones played for fools. They tried to beat their religion out of them and turn them into Christians because they feared what they did not understand and did not know. It backfired on them! They took away the drums because they feared them. The elders didn't need drums in order to worship; foot stomp and the clapping of hands worked just as well. They forced the ancestors to be Christians, not understanding that they were going to find a way to still worship. They handed them the power and didn't even realize it because they were so arrogant and self-serving, but after all the hardships, after everything that the ancestors went through, they still managed to survive.

I didn't include the whole spiritual. I simply want to show you the secrets and the messages that are hidden within the spiritual's lyrics. The first line says, "When the sun comes back, and the first quail calls." We know that the sun rises early in the morning, and quails are active early in the morning, so the song lets us know that the time to leave is early in the morning.

It goes on to tell us that we are going to be going along the river because it says, "the river bank makes a mighty good road."

So if you look at the next line, it actually tells us what to look for. We are going to follow the path where there is a line of dead trees. Then it says, "Left foot, peg foot, travelin' on," so we are going to move forward and take the left-handed path until we come to a smaller path.

It goes on to tell us that we are going to come to two hills, and when we see those hills we're going to know that a river has run out. But because of the stanza that says, "Follow the drinkin' gourd," we know that we're going to keep moving.

Then it tells us that even though we ran out of river there's another river on the other side of those hills, so we just keep it moving. We keep going until we run into the great river that meets the little river. Once we get where the two rivers meet, there is going to be an old fella there who is going to take us to freedom. He's there waiting for us just to make it to him.

I didn't live back in that day, so I can't swear to any of this. The only thing I know for sure is that I trust my elders and I believe in what they've taught me and what I've learned. There is so much information that is hidden and is being lost today. We need more elders. We need more folks who have been taught the work hands-on. This work should not be able to just die off. It has been passed down for generations, through families, and the ancestors of this work deserve to live on.

I was going to stop here, but I think I'm going to do one more. These are stories that need to be told. The courage that it took to survive in slavery cannot ever be overlooked, and the wisdom and the intelligence that it took to get through it.

"Wrestling Jacob"

Not every spiritual is about getting away. Sometimes it's about death, like the spiritual "Wrestling Jacob." If you look up the lyrics to this spiritual, we see the time of day is daybreak, when the sun is coming up. The lyrics go on to say that Jacob is holding onto his brother and his sister and he doesn't want to let them go. We learn that he was hung from a trembling limb and that the slaver would not let him go. In the last line he asks God to bless his soul.

This spiritual tells a story of someone being killed, and from the story we can tell that there were other folks made to watch this, because it's said that he held on to his brother and his sister and he did not want to let them go. He did not want to leave them.

We can never forget the horrors of slavery or the people who suffered at the hands of the slavers. I can't even imagine living through hell like that. This is why I write my books. The ancestors deserve to be remembered and to be honored. I hope that this helps you to understand the secret meanings and messages in some of these spirituals.

2

The Ancestors

Honoring your ancestors is not worshipping them. I had someone tell me one time that it was against God's will for me to worship my ancestors. Honoring and worshipping are two different things. If you look in the Bible to see what it says about honoring the ancestors, the most you will find in there is warnings against worshipping the dead. I think that this is one reason Christians have a problem with Conjure. They don't understand.

There is a big difference between honoring and worshipping. I don't get on my knees when I honor my ancestors; I don't bow down to them. I offer prayers for them, I thank them for the things that they went through in their lives to get me where I am today. It is not the same as worshipping them. When you worship something, you bow down, you get on your knees. My ancestors would never expect me to bow down to them or to any man.

Folks tend to fear things that they do not understand. The same types of Christians don't understand that every time they go to the graveyard, and they place flowers on the graves of their loved ones, they are honoring the dead. Every holiday that they go to the graveyard, and they dress those graves, they are honoring the dead. This is no different than what folks do who venerate their ancestors; it's the same thing. Perception really is everything.

Serving our ancestors really has nothing to do with religion, but it is considered a religious expression. That's where the problem comes in with most Christians, because the ones who I have run into believe that honoring the ancestors and worshipping them is the same thing. I personally do not believe this; I believe that if it were not for our ancestors and what they went through, we wouldn't be where we are today. Because of their trials and tribulations, they have made it better for each generation to prosper and to grow.

The basis of serving our ancestors stems from the belief that the spirits of the dead continue to dwell in the natural world and have the power to influence the fortune and fate of the living. It is believed that ancestors can assert their powers by blessing or cursing. They are also regarded as the intermediaries between the living and the divine powers. In general, ancestors are believed to wield great authority, having special powers to influence the course of events or to control the well-being of their descendants. Helping and keeping the family safe is one of their main concerns.

The serving of ancestors has been found in various parts of the world. All societies give ritual attention to death or to the souls of the dead, but not all of these practices are called serving our ancestors. They have different names in different countries. As Conjure workers, it is our job to take care of the spirits that walk with us, and that includes our ancestors.

Our ancestors are always regarded with respect, and we continue to have a bond with them even though they have passed on. We still love them, we feel joy when we think of them, and we miss them. The bond was not severed when they passed on, because we have our memories of them.

I was taught to believe that as long as you hold someone in your heart they still live on. The spirits see, hear, feel, understand, and communicate with the living; they make moral judgments; they are wishful, willful, joyful, angry, stern, permissive, kind, and cruel; they have all the emotions and traits of human beings. Don't be fooled, though. If your ancestor was a horrible person when they were alive, they haven't changed; they are still that same miserable, horrible person even after they have passed on to the other side.

If your ancestor was a loving person when they walked among the living, they still hold that trait. If they were cruel and heartless, those emotions will still be there. Just because they have passed on doesn't mean they have changed their ways. That's why it is important that you call on the ancestors you know who loved you and will be happy to help you with your needs.

This is where I need to put in a word of caution: when you are dealing with spirits (even your ancestors), you have to be mindful, and you have to use discernment when you are calling on them. There are some elders who believe that you shouldn't even honor your ancestors unless you have experience doing so. That's because if you don't have experience, how can you be sure that the spirit you are calling in is really an ancestor? It could be a malevolent spirit.

There are a couple of ways that you can honor your ancestors. You can set up an altar in your home for them, or you can honor them on holidays and birthdays by going to the graveyard and taking care of their graves. I know this may be new to some folks if you were not raised in the southern culture. I have to remind myself often that not everybody was raised like I was raised, and not everybody knows what I know, but I really want folks to know how to honor their dead so I'm going to take my time and explain how to set up an altar and also how to tend to the graves of your loved ones. We will start with tending to the graves of your loved ones.

Tending to Your Ancestors' Graves

Every year my family goes to the graveyard and tends to the graves of our people—sometimes more than once a year. When you are doing anything in the graveyard, you need to be very respectful. The graveyard can be a dangerous place if you are not careful. It is not a place to play around with. Not only do you have the spirits of the dead who are buried there, but you also have spirits roaming around.

When you enter a graveyard, you should always pay the spirit at the gate when you go in and when you come out. Different workers will tell you a different amount to drop at the gate. I keep change in the console of my car so I always have some ready, because you never know when you're going to need it. I will simply grab some change and drop it at the front gate when I go into the graveyard; when I come out, I will drop some more.

If you decide to honor your kin at their graves, then you need to bring a few items with you: a bucket, water, rags, spiritual water—it could be Florida Water or holy water—an offering of flowers or other gifts, and ammonia. Once you've located your loved one's grave, wash the headstone with the rags and water. Clean it well while saying prayers for your loved one. Once the headstone is clean, add some of the Florida Water or holy water to your bucket of clean water and go back over the headstone again. Next, place your flowers or gifts on top of the grave.

My mama liked to drink black coffee and smoke Pall Mall cigarettes, so I will bring her black coffee and give her cigarettes when I visit her. My daddy, on the other hand, liked to drink whiskey and smoke cigars, so I'll bring him whiskey and give him a cigar.

Whatever liquid I am giving I pour directly on top of the grave. I sit there and talk to them just like they were still here. If I have a problem, I tell them all about it. Whatever is going on at the time, I discuss it with them. I always feel better after I visit them at the grave.

The old folks believe that when you leave the graveyard you should clean yourself off so that you don't bring any spirits home with you. You can do this by wiping your shoes off with some ammonia.

Just remember that the graveyard is nowhere to play around. I can't stress this enough. I had someone email me not too long ago asking for my help because they felt like they had picked up a spirit in the graveyard. In the email they told me that they had partied in the graveyard. They had had a sexual encounter in the graveyard, and they had gotten married in the graveyard. It boggles my mind, the disrespect that folks have for the dead. This makes no sense to me. I told them that I was unable to help them and referred them to my godfather.

If you don't respect your ancestors and the dead, then you don't respect yourself. Be mindful of the things that you do and how you act when you're serving your dead in the graveyard. It's really not a place to play and party and have fun. Spirits are very real, and they can be very dangerous. Like my mama always told us, "Spirits can't hurt you, but they can make you hurt yourself." That always stuck with me. But I was raised to respect and honor my dead kin, folks, and the dead in general.

Creating an Ancestor Altar

Now let's look at putting an altar together. Some folks like to go over-board with their altars and they set up these large, elaborate altars. That's fine. If you have the space to do so, then I think it's a great idea. But your altar could also be small, and it could even be hidden. No matter how you choose to make your altar, remember that the old saying, "Cleanliness is next to godliness," applies when you're dealing with spirit. They are not going to want to be somewhere that is not clean. We'll talk more about altars in a later chapter, but here is a basic overview for now.

Basic Altar Setup

The first step is to figure out where you want to set up your altar, and whether it is going to be a permanent altar or just a space that you are going to utilize once a week to honor your ancestors. It depends on your lifestyle and the space you have in your home.

Once you decide on the space and the table or whatever you're going to use to set the altar on, then you need to clean that area. Some folks will set their altars on the floor, which is perfectly fine if you don't have animals or small children. You need to make you a wash, whether that's a little bit of ammonia or brown Lysol, and clean the area well. Wipe off the table, clean the floor, and if you have wood walls, wipe the walls down. While you are doing this, you should be thinking about your ancestors and inviting them into your home.

Once you have everything clean, let it air-dry. Then you need to decide what type of cloth you are going to put on the table. There are a couple of different ways you can set up this altar.

One way is to just have a table with a nice cloth. On it, you'll place a candle, water, and a cup of coffee once a week. You can also put things on there that your dead loved in life, things that they liked. I've seen folks put fine china that belonged to their grandmother on there—a sin-gle serving. You could also give them fresh flowers once a week. You can add whatever you want to your altar.

I personally honor my ancestors on Mondays; it's the beginning of the week and a fresh start for the new work week. There is really no set day, though—you can choose the day that fits into your schedule. Make sure that you keep that space clean for them once you set it up. It becomes a holy place.

Hidden Altars

I have never hidden what I do and how I live, but I do understand that there are certain situations in life when you have to hide things in plain sight for whatever reason. If you have nosey family members or folks in your life who might not approve of this work, then you can simply hide the altar. It's easy to do.

You follow the same instructions on setting up your space as if it were an altar in plain sight, but you simply turn the table into a family photo table. Don't put the living with the dead, though. You can take the photos of your dead kin and put them in some nice frames, along with any special items that they've given you. Place them on the table. You can also take a good-smelling candle (it doesn't have to be a spiritual candle) and light it on the table for them. When no one is around, you can offer them coffee and a cool glass of water. Leave these things there for a little while and then pick them up.

No one has to know that you have an ancestor altar, and no one will know unless you tell them, because it's going to just look like a nice table that you have put together with your family on it. There is always more than one way to skin a cat. Remember, you don't have to always announce to the world what you're doing.

There is no set way to do an altar—it's very personal. When it comes down to it, the most important thing is that you are remembering and honoring your ancestors. I don't believe that they really care what the altar looks like or even if you have an altar—it's how you honor them and remember them that counts. Altars help us more than they help spirit. Altars give us a place to focus, a place to sit at, a place to pour our heart out at. Spirit is always with us. They walk with us daily, so we don't have to go sit at a table to call them, because they are always with us. It is more for our benefit than it is for theirs.

Servicing Your Ancestors

You can service your spirits by simply pouring libations on the ground for them and telling them, "This is the offering for you. I'm honoring you for everything that you do for me." They don't have to have a lot of elaborate hocus pocus going on in order for them to know how much we love and appreciate them—that's more for us than it is for spirit. So don't get stressed out, and don't overthink it. Just follow your heart and do whatever you can do in order to serve your spirits.

Sometimes we stress ourselves out because we look at what other folks are doing and how they're serving their spirits and we feel like we need to follow suit. This is absolutely not true. You do you—do the best that you can. Use discernment and listen to your spirits. They'll tell you when they need more. They'll let you know. Just don't get stressed out about it. That's not what this is all about. Like my mama used to say, "Don't try to keep up with the Joneses. Let the Joneses tend to their own stoop, and you tend to yours."

Saying Your Prayers

Before doing any type of spiritual work, you need to first say your prayers. I usually say three Our Fathers, three Hail Marys, and three Apostles' Creeds (you'll find these in the back of this book). Then I follow through with my personal prayer. A personal prayer comes from your heart, and it's however you feel when you're praying. No one can tell you what to say.

I have realized over the years that not everybody knows how to pray. If you really don't know how to pray, then just speak from your heart. The spirits are going to listen to you no matter what. This is very important. If you don't know how to do this, then you can call on your guardian angel to protect you. We all have a guardian angel that has been with us since birth. You have other spirits that walk with you that have been with you your whole life too. Don't worry about who they are; just know that they are there and they have always been there, and they watch over you and take care of you.

Prayer before any type of work is very important because you are calling on the unknown. You are lighting candles, which draws in spirits. You are offering libations, which pulls in spirits. And not all spirits are good spirits or have your best interests at heart. I'm not trying to scare you—I'm just trying to make you aware that doing spiritual work is a serious thing, and you have to take it seriously. It's not a game. It's not something that you play around with. It's the real deal. So just be mindful. Pay attention to what you're doing, and use discernment when it comes to the way you pray and what you ask for.

Praying is a very important part of this work. This is how you interact with spirit. This is how you get your petitions to spirit. All of it is done through prayer. It may seem like a lot of work, but in the long run the benefits of being close to your spirits and taking care of your spirits outweighs the time it takes to say your prayers daily and to honor your spirits.

Some folks like to set a lot of rules about how you do this and how you do that, but nobody can tell you how to serve your spirits and your ancestors. That is something that is very personal and very private. The serving of our ancestors consists of the lighting of candles, prayers, presenting gifts, and making offerings. In my family, we honor our dead by cleaning and dressing their graves for holidays. They can and will remove all obstacles that may be in your path. All you have to do is call upon them to come to your aid.

Get to know your ancestors. Build a relationship with them, and remember that all ancestors are not necessarily blood-related. I have elders that I include on my altar because they are like family to me. They were in my life and they mean something to me. So it's not always blood kinfolk that is an ancestor, and it's not always blood kinfolk that's going to have your best interest at heart from the spirit world. Just do the best that you can to take it slow and easy. Just do the work and you will be rewarded for your efforts. And remember, everything that you do, you and you alone are responsible for it.

3

Working with Spirit

The Bible is a contradiction whenever it comes to spirits and contacting them and listening to them. In some places, it says that to deal with any type of spirits you are dealing with demons; and yet, in other places, it talks about where the spirit of the Lord came down and talked to the prophet Isaiah, talked to Moses, talked to St. Peter . . . so which is it? This is why discernment is so important, so you know what type of spirit you are dealing with.

What the Bible Tells Us about Working with Spirit

The Bible tells us that there are all kinds of spirits, and it also tells us that dealing with most of them is a sin. First, you have the holy spirits: the spirit of wisdom, the spirit of understanding, the spirit of knowledge, and the spirit of faith. So where exactly do these spirits come from? How do they find us? How do we know that they're real? The gift of discernment is just that—a gift—and like any gift, in order for it to grow, you have to work with it. You should never follow anyone or anything blindly.

If someone tells you something, you should be able to ask questions about what they're telling you. If they don't want to answer your questions, then I wouldn't mess with them at all. You know, growing up, my mama would tell us to do something. If we said, "Why?" She would say,

"Because I told you to do it." Well, that's my mother, and I was a child. I'm no longer a child. So I want to know why I'm doing certain things—especially when you're dealing with spirits.

You have to learn that it's OK to ask a spirit to give you a sign that what they are telling you to do is the right thing to do and that it's coming from the right type of spirit. Don't ever just jump into this work with both feet. You take your time, you learn. I've been doing this work since I was seventeen years old. That's when I first learned how to do cleansings on my oldest boy, because he was sick all the time. The old *padrino* (godfather) explained to me what I was doing and why I was doing it and what the effect of it was supposed to be. He didn't just give me a set of instructions and tell me what to do; he explained the steps, he watched me do the work. If I had a question, I could ask him.

If you look at Isaiah 11: 2-3 (New International Version), this is what it says:

2 The Spirit of the Lord will rest on him.

I take that to mean that the spirit of the Lord walks with me. It goes on to say,

the Spirit of wisdom and of understanding,

the Spirit of counsel and of might,

the Spirit of the knowledge and fear of the Lord.

3 and he will delight in the fear of the Lord.

He will not judge by what he sees with his eyes,

or decide by what he hears with his ears;

Let's look at that for a minute. "He will not judge by what he sees with his eyes." So this right here tells me that the only thing that you can judge is what spirit has shown you. Then it goes on, "or decide by what he hears." Once again I believe that it is telling us we should believe what spirit shows us.

Like I said earlier, the Bible is a contradiction. You have to use discernment when you are reading it. Here's an example. If you look in Leviticus 19:26, you will see that God said, "You will not practice divination or soothsaying." And yet he has given the gift of sight to many:

> *"Do not eat any meat with the blood still in it.*
> *"Do not practice divination or seek omens.*

You will find quite a few verses where the prophets talk about magic being against God's will and fortune-telling being against God's will. This is where the contradiction comes in, because within the Bible—the Old Testament and the New Testament—you will find chapters and verses that talk about casting lots as a way of finding out who should get what. Even when Jesus was crucified, they divided up his clothes by casting lots (Matthew 27:35)

Let's look at a few more. I feel like it's important that we look at the whole picture and not just a piece of the picture. A lot of Christians preach that it's a sin to do divination, and yet the Bible is full of casting lots to get answers to important questions. If you look at Jonah 1:7, it tells us that they cast the lots to see why they were having so much trouble. Unfortunately, it fell on Jonah. So that let them know that something was going on with Jonah for all this trouble to fall on him:

> *Then the sailors said to each other, "Come, let us cast lots to find out who is responsible for this calamity." They cast lots and the lot fell on Jonah.*

Before we go further, what exactly is the casting of lots? From talking to old folks, it seems that small sticks were cut and then thrown either on the ground or on a white cloth. So, from what I understand, it's really not that much different from throwing the bones or reading stones. Yet today's preachers preach against it when they claim that God speaks to him. We have to always remember that churches are built and run by man.

In Nehemiah 11:1, we see that they threw lots to see who would live in Jerusalem and who would live somewhere else:

> *Now the leaders of the people settled in Jerusalem. The rest of the people cast lots to bring one out of every ten of them to live in Jerusalem, the holy city, while the remaining nine were to stay in their own towns.*

For me, this shows me just how important the throwing of lots was.

I want to do one more, and then we're going to move on. I'm just not going to tell you something without showing you, though.

If you look at Joshua 18:8, it tells us that Joshua sent a group of men out to survey the land. When these men came back, Joshua threw the lots to see which land God wanted:

> *As the men started on their way to map out the land, Joshua instructed them, "Go and make a survey of the land and write a description of it. Then return to me, and I will cast lots for you here at Shiloh in the presence of the Lord."*

Because he said he was throwing the lots before the Lord in Shiloh, we are given the gift of sight and the gift of discernment to be utilized. To not use our gifts is to deny God, and the Bible strictly says you should never deny God.

I just feel like there are too many contradictions and bone-picking when it comes to the Bible and some of these preachers. You can't have your cake and eat it too, as old folks say. You can't say it's wrong to use divination if God gives you that gift but it's OK to prophecy in church. It is basically the same thing. One you're using a tool, the other you're speaking whatever God put on you to speak. It's the same thing.

There are many children born with the gift of sight, but growing up that gift is not looked upon as a gift—it's looked upon as something evil. But getting the Bible, it says that God gives some folks the gift of sight and the gift of discernment. So if God gave it to us, how can it be evil? Because the people of the church say it is. Instead of scaring them, they should be lifting them up and letting their gifts grow.

Growing Your Gift of Discernment

When I was growing up and someone was cutting up or acting real jealous, my elders would say that they had the spirit of jealousy on them. Even the Bible talks about the spirit of jealousy.

Jealousy comes in many forms, and I was raised to believe that jealousy is a devil or a demon. This is where discernment comes in really well, because when you're around folks and they start acting a certain way, you need to be able to see, Is this just a one-time thing? Or do they really have a jealous spirit? The thing that I have learned about folks who are jealous in my own life is that they want to be close to you, and maybe part of them loves you, but the other part despises you and your gifts and your blessings. I have learned that you really need to watch out for these types of folks. They are the type who would do whatever it takes to build themselves up and make themselves look good while in the background they are gossiping and telling falsehoods about you. Be very mindful of the flow you deal with. Watch them. Listen to the words that come out of their mouth and the actions that tell the real truth. I just want to go through a few of these before moving on.

The next one I want to look at is the lying spirit. These folks cannot tell the truth to save their life. They constantly heap falsehoods, and the problem is that most of the time these types of folks are so good at it, and have done it for so long, that people truly believe the lies they tell. These types of folks are very dangerous—especially if they have a voice out in the public. Anytime you are dealing with any type of people, you need the strong gift of discernment—and you need to learn to follow that discernment and not your heart.

I have known folks in my life who I love dearly and I still held on to even though I knew that they had been lying, cheating, or jealous. I overlooked it—and in the long run it wasn't good. So make sure that when you are dealing with people that you truly use your gift of discernment (*Really, what are they all about?*) before you get in too deep with them. You can like someone and keep them at arm's length; you can like someone and be around them; but when folks have these types of ailments, for your own safety you should always be watchful.

St. Clare is the saint to go to when you are trying to build your gift of discernment. St. Clare has the gift of sight, and she can help you make your gifts stronger. She will also show you things that are hidden. She has a nine-day novena that you can do. I'm not adding it here, but you can find it online.

St. Clare Working

To work with St. Clare to build up your gift of sight and discernment, you will need a white candle and a glass of water. You should do this work daily. Light your candle and say your normal prayers that you usually say.

When I pray, I pray three Our Fathers, then three Hail Marys, and three Apostles' Creeds. (I know that not everybody is Catholic or even knows where to find these prayers, so I've included them in the back of the book.) Then you say your personal prayer and petition the Holy Trinity, which is God the Father, God the Son, and God the Holy Spirit, to help with your gift of discernment.

Then you move on to St. Clare's novena. Ask that St. Clare intercede and help you build your gift of discernment so that you may see all the things that you need to see to help you along in your life. You will repeat this prayer and petition three times every time you pray.

Ideally, you would do this three times a day, but I know in this day and age very few have time, so just do the set of prayers once a day if you have to.

Once you have finished with your prayers, put the candle out. Save it for the next day. Pour the water out on the ground and give thanks to the spirit for helping you. Then you simply repeat the process daily, and before you know it, things that you see are going to start changing. They're going to be more clear.

4

Is Conjure a Religion?

Conjure is not a religion, per se, although it does have religious aspects to it. When the slave trade started and the ancestors were brought over here and placed on plantations, they were not allowed to practice their religions. The white slave owners feared them. It was against the law for them to gather and worship, so everything they did they had to hide from the folks that owned the plantations. They had no privacy whatsoever. They were basically watched every minute of the day. I'm sure that this did not stop them from gathering in secret and from worshipping, but it put a damper on it. If they got caught gathering, they could have been beaten, maimed, or even killed. The whites who owned the enslaved people literally made it a crime for them to practice their religion. Most of the time they were forced to become Christian.

Even though they had been removed from the continent and brought over here, they still held on to their religious beliefs. If you have ever been to an African American church, you will notice the difference between that church and white American churches. The worship services are very different, and the teachings are somewhat different.

One of my elders told me one time—this was before the internet and all of this—that Conjure workers are a special kind of Christian. We are not the run-of-the-mill Bible-thumping Christians; we look at the Bible and prayer differently than a regular Christian. We understand that there's a right hand and there's the left hand, and sometimes when you're doing this work you have to work with both hands.

Conjure work is not all love and light. You cannot have light without having darkness, and Conjure workers understand that. Even the Bible is not all love and light.

I personally consider myself a Christian, but I also look at the world as a Conjure worker. I believe that all work, be it light or dark, can be done if it's justified. Even though Conjure work is not a religion, I believe that the Bible plays a large part in it. I feel like the ancestors knew what they were doing, and even though they were not allowed to totally worship because of slavery, they made it work for them.

A lot of these works have been passed down from generation to generation within families. These are things that I was raised with and went on to learn from other elders. This is how I've raised my children and my grandchildren. This is how we live. I don't go to church every Sunday. I believe that churches are man-made and that a lot of the rules of the church are man-made. But I do pray every day and I do work my Bible every day. It's the way I live. It's my life. So even though Conjure is not a religion, the Bible does play a large part in it.

PART II

Getting Started

There are three key elements to doing Conjure work: One is the prayer and petition that you put into the work; the second is the ingredients that go into the work; and the third puts it all in spirit's hands.

I have learned over the years doing this work that the path of least resistance is the best way to go if you are looking for success in your work. I truly believe that when you have to fight, scratch, and dig for something, then that something is not for you, because whatever is for you is going to be for you, and it's going to be easy to reach that goal.

Sometimes it seems like things just drag out and take forever to get to where they're supposed to be. In my world, when this happens, I look at the whole situation. I see the work I'm doing. What else could I be doing to help push the work along? Because I believe that in order to have success and to be a successful worker, you have to do more than one thing to achieve that success.

In the next few chapters, we're going to look at these key elements of Conjure work—setting up an altar to honor the ancestors, practicing divination before doing any working, offering prayer, preparing offerings for the ancestors, and using the arms of the cross.

5

How I Learned

Nowadays, learning Conjure is different than when I began learning at seventeen years old. When I first got taught how to do cleansing work at seventeen, it was out of necessity to help my child who was very ill. Looking back over all the elders I have had, I realize that each one of them came to me in a time when I needed them. My mama raised us a certain way and she did things a certain way. It was just a way of life for us growing up. So I already had a foundation in Conjure even though I didn't know it was Conjure.

You see, when I was coming up, my mama just did whatever she did and there wasn't a name on it. When we would come in from outside, we took our shoes off at the door. That was every day of our lives. She picked up our shoes and wiped them off. Now I know that she wiped them off with a wet rag and turpentine, because I know what turpentine smells like. She didn't say, "Oh, I'm doing Conjure. I'm doing magic." She didn't say that. But this is something that she did every single day.

All the things that she did that became part of our life came from the way she was raised and the culture that she was raised in. She raised us in that same culture. She never talked about why she did whatever she was doing. No explanation for the things that she did every day. So that gave me a strong foundation to begin with, because it's my culture. It's the way I was raised. It's not something I studied, it's not something somebody taught me—it's my whole life.

When I was growing up, sometimes I would feel a little some kind of way about my mama. Not in a bad way, but just that I wished that she was more like other people's mamas. But she wasn't. She had her own ways of doing things that set her apart from my friends' mothers. When you're young, sometimes some things seem odd, and some of the things my mama did seemed odd at the time, but now I understand and I do the same odd things.

If you can find an elder to take you in, that is the best way to learn this work. But you're going to have to search for them. You need to really watch them, see how they interact with other folks, see what they're teaching. Make sure that they're not mixing Conjure with other things to fill in the voids for things that they don't know. With the internet nowadays, there's a teacher on every corner. Does that mean that they know what they're doing? No, it doesn't. The best teachers are going to be the ones who are raised in the southern culture! I'm not talking bad about nobody. I'm not slinging salt. I'm just saying that if you want to find a good elder, you need to find an elder who was raised in this culture. And the best way to do that is to get to know people before you jump in with both feet.

If you can't find an elder, then the next best thing is to take some classes and read some books that are written by folks who were raised in the Southern culture. I'm sure this is going to upset some folks, and that's OK. We know what they say about opinions (everyone has them, like a certain something else), but someone who was not raised in the Southern culture is not going to understand the culture. The food is different. The way we are raised is different. The old wives' tales are different. The way we live is different. Southern children are raised from birth to be respectful of their elders and to be respectful of themselves. Be respectful of the culture. Learn about the culture. Learn about the people. Learn everything that you can learn about the way the people live. This is how you start.

Here's the part where I shamelessly tell you that two of the best books to start with are my own: *Old Style Conjure* and *Hoodoo Herbal*. Both of those would be great for a beginner, someone who is not familiar with Conjure. They would also be great for the seasoned worker. But if you can't get those two books for whatever reason, I'm going to share a little information that will help you get started, a few steps you can work with that will help open the door.

Cleansing

The first thing, which is very important, because I have found that folks don't keep themselves spiritually cleansed, is to talk about cleansing. I'm just going to touch on it here so it'll all be in one place that's easy for you to find, even though I go into detail about this in other places in this book.

Cleansing Yourself

The easiest way to do a cleansing is what I call an egg cleansing. Most of us have eggs in our Frigidaire. You need to take the egg out, set it on the counter, and let it become room temperature. You also need a glass of cool water and two pieces of broom straw right out of your broom. (The glass needs to be made of glass, not plastic. I have found that plastic doesn't work because you can't see through it.)

To start the cleansing, start with the egg at the top of your head. Move the egg, going downward and outward. Make sure to clean the bottoms of your feet going from heel to toe. The egg will literally change the way it feels in your hand; it will start to feel a little heavy. When you are done with the cleansing, crack the egg into the glass of water. Then place the two pieces of broom straw in the shape of a cross on top of the water. The reason that I was told to put the egg in water is 1) so we can read the condition of the egg; and 2) because the water holds down whatever we have taken off of our body when we cleansed it with the egg. The broom straw is placed on top of the water in the shape of the cross to keep whatever came off locked down. Let the egg sit in the water for three hours, and then dispose of it. When I'm working with an egg for cleansing, I like to give the egg back to the earth. The earth heals.

Cleansing Your Home

To clean your home, you can roll an egg gently from room to room, all the way to the front door. Then you take that egg and you go throw it in the crossroads. This is an easy way to do a house cleansing. The egg is going to pick up a lot of what is there. Just be gentle or you'll end up with a broken egg.

Protecting Your Home

The next thing I want to touch on—and these are important things that we need in our everyday lives as workers—is protection of the home. Of course, there are stronger things that you can do to protect your home, but right now I just want to give you some things that you can do to protect your home until you can find someone to either help you or learn more on your own.

The first thing is to get a glass bowl. Put salt in the bowl, then cut a lime and place half of the lime on top of the salt. Put the bowl behind the front door of your home or apartment. This will help cut any negative energies that folks might bring into your home. Change the lime out once a week.

The next thing that you can do to help protect your home is to place small mirrors in the windows that are facing the street.

Another easy thing that you can do is place a small broom by the door with the head of the broom facing downward. It will help clear out anything that's not supposed to be in your house. Once a week, you can take that broom and brush the inside and the outside of your door to clear away anything that might be there. Then you just hang your broom back by the door.

I believe that the ancestors held on to as much as they possibly could from their homeland, and it shows when you look at the way we are taught to sweep the floors. Sweeping may be a simple thing for some folks, but in my world it is a big thing. When I was growing up, we were not allowed to play with the broom. My mama would not allow it. My grandma used to sweep her yard, and she is really the one who taught me how to sweep. And I have to be honest, it was a hard lesson, because I was a kid and I didn't understand the difference between moving the broom back and forth and sweeping in one sweep. There is a big difference—and now that I'm grown and have had elders of my own, I understand why you don't sweep back and forth. It also has bled over into Conjure work, because when you sweep your home when you're cleansing it you sweep in one direction. If you're doing cleansing work and you're working with a broom, you sweep in one direction from top to bottom, going downward. If you sweep back and forth, all you are doing is stirring up whatever you're trying to get rid of and giving it a chance to run into a corner somewhere. This is a part of Conjure work and it came from the ancestors.

Another way that you can protect your home is to put bay leaves in the corners of each room of your home.

Praying Every Day

Get into the habit of praying every day. I have learned that some folks don't know how to pray. You simply speak the words. If you are a beginner, start with a cool glass of water and a stick candle. Light your candle, then say three Our Fathers, three Hail Marys, and three Apostles' Creeds. Then add your personal prayer and a petition if there's something that you need to have brought into your life. It may seem strange at first if you're not used to praying every day, but this is actually going to make you a stronger worker.

And Remember . . .

Just take your time. Go slow because it's not a race. It has literally taken me fifty years to get where I am today. The knowledge that I have I have learned from numerous elders over the last fifty years. Each one of them taught me something that helped me go further in my work. That's the best advice I can give you—take your time, learn the culture, learn about the people of the culture. Learn where this work comes from.

6

Setting Up an Altar

The very first step is to decide if you really need or want an altar set up in your home. Altars are a lot of work once you set them up; you are responsible for keeping the altar clean and you are responsible for taking care of the spirits that sit on that altar. You cannot just set up an altar and leave it there. That altar has to be served and it has to be kept clean. Those are your spirits sitting on that altar, and you are responsible for them and the altar. So don't jump into this with both feet; really think about it and then move forward.

You don't have to have an altar to honor your spirits. You could simply give them a candle, some refreshments, and maybe a food offering every once in a while, and this can simply be set outside in a nice space. Or you could cleanse a space in your home and simply have an altar up for the day. It's really up to you. I just want you to understand that this is a lot of responsibility.

Different religions look at altars differently. Conjure is not a religion, so the same thing does not apply. Having an altar in Conjure work is a place for you to do your work, a place for you to focus on, and it's also a place that will build power over time. Conjure work is not Vodou, Santeria, Palo, or any other religion, because Conjure work is not a religion—it's magic. The same rules working an altar does not apply to Conjure as it does to a religious altar, such as a Vodou altar. They are two completely different things.

Nowadays, folks try to blend everything into one pot. Conjure work is Conjure work; it's magic. It can be confusing to folks who don't know the difference, so I'm going to repeat what I said: Conjure is not a religion, and it does not have the religious structure that Vodou, Santeria, Palo, or other religions have. It is a set of magical works.

Building Your Altar

If you decide that you do want an altar, then the first step is to figure out where you want to place it. Then you'll cleanse and assemble your items.

Altar Placement

As a young worker, I was advised not to set up an altar in my bedroom, because when you are working that altar and you have candles and stuff burning, you are drawing spirit into that area—and sometimes it's not only the spirits you are working with, but other spirits that are drawn to the energies and the power coming out of that altar. I understand that the way it is today, some folks might not have any other place to put their altar besides in their bedroom. If this is the case, then I would advise covering the altar at night when you are asleep. When you are asleep, you have no defense against unwanted spirits coming in. You're basically helpless. So just to be on the safe side, blow all the candles out and cover the altar with a dark cloth.

Once you have found your space where you want to place the altar, you need to spiritually cleanse the space with a spiritual wash. You will also need to cleanse the table that the altar will be sitting on with the same wash. Everything needs to be cleansed, dressed, and blessed. You can't "just throw something" together, because the altar is a holy place.

Cleansing Wash

To cleanse the area, make a wash with basil, three bay leaves, and olive leaves. These are all holy herbs. You make the wash the same way you steep a cup of tea, except this is a spiritual wash and it needs to be prayed over so spirit can come down into the wash.

Once you have your water in your pot with the fire going, you need to start saying your prayers. You need to say three Our Fathers, three

Hail Marys, and three Glory Bes (these are in the back of the book). Once you've said your starting prayers, then you can move on to your personal prayer. You should ask spirit to guide you and lead you and walk with you while you are making this cleansing wash.

Once that is done, you need to pick up each herb one at a time and say your petition over it. Then place the herb in the pot with the water. Once all the herbs are in the pot, using a wooden spoon, stir the water going in the opposite direction of the clock. You do this three times, so remember where you first started to stir. When you are going in the opposite direction of the hands of the clock, you are petitioning to remove all negative energies that those herbs might have picked up from folks handling them before you got them.

Then you're going to go three times in the direction of the hands of the clock. When you change the direction and you start going in the direction of the hands of the clock, you petition spirit to fill that wash with the power to clear away all negative energies and to draw in blessing.

Once the wash has come to a full boil, turn the fire off, put the lid on the pot, and let the wash steep.

Once the wash is cool, it is ready to use. Pour it into a container. Get a white cloth and wipe down the whole area where the altar will be, and also clean off the table or shelf that the altar will sit on. Let the altar air-dry.

And since you already have the wash made, you could use the rest of that wash to wipe down your door inside and out, and you could clean your stoop. Don't waste that wash. It can be added to your mop water to mop your house. A little could be added to the laundry to bless the clothes. You could even wash the sidewalk down leading away from your home to remove any negative energies that might have been in place.

Assembling Your Altar

When your area is clean and dry, then it's time to decide what you are going to place on this altar. You need some type of cloth to cover the altar with; you need a Bible that you can place on your altar to work with doing bibliomancy; you need a glass; and you need a candle. This is the basic altar.

If you find this altar too boring, you can add other things. You can place flowers on the altar. You can place spiritual statues on the altar. You can place whatever you want on that altar because that altar is yours. An altar is very personal. No one can tell you what your altar should be; that is between you and the spirits that walk with you. The altar can be as plain or as elaborate as you need it to be! It all depends on your taste. Spirit will come when you call them no matter what you have the altar sitting on or how it is set up. Don't overthink this. You will grow over time.

Using Your Altar

You can sit by the altar and just speak to your spirits. I know some folks like to make folks think there's a lot of hocus pocus to it, but there really isn't. It's so simple, it seems to be too good to be true. If Conjure was a religion, then there would be steps you need to take to approach spirit and to work the altar, but it isn't—it's magic.

I work my altars daily, but I am a professional worker. You need to pick at least one day a week where you can spend time at your altar. This is the time when you talk to your spirits about whatever is going on in your world. This is the day to give them a fresh glass of cool water and a light—the water and candle not only feed spirit, but also draw spirit into the space.

If you have a problem going on in your life, then you can go straight to your altar and speak with your spirits that sit there and petition them for their help. Remember to always say your prayers and call on spirits that walk with you for protection before you do any type of work—even just sitting at your altar talking to your spirits. Also remember that your altar is a holy place and should be treated as such.

7

Divination

Divination is an important part of this work. It's a way for us to be able to listen to what spirit is trying to tell us. It's vital that you be able to divine a situation before you decide what to do with it or how to fix it. This gift of sight is a gift from God; if it wasn't, we wouldn't have it. No matter how you divine your answers—throwing bones, reading cards, interpreting dreams, using a pendulum, or another method—you need to make sure you are honoring your ancestors and your practice in the process.

Divination and the Bible

A lot of Conjure workers work with the Bible doing bibliomancy, which is the practice of divining using the Bible. To work with the Bible in divination, all you have to do is hold the Bible between the palms of your hands, blow three breaths on the Bible, and petition God to give you the answer that you are looking for. Repeat your petition three times. Then open the Bible up and read the first section that your eyes fall on. If you don't understand the passage or what spirit is trying to tell you, then repeat the process, but this time petition the spirit to give you the answer in a way that you will understand what they are trying to tell you. Discernment plays a big part in bibliomancy. You have to be able to understand what you are reading and put it together.

I know a lot of churchgoing folks will tell you that divination is against God's law. This is absolutely not true, and I'm going to show you places in the Bible where divination is used to figure things out. The Bible is a powerful tool and it is a powerful book in Conjure. If you are looking for answers, you can find them with a Bible. For example, the Bible talks about the throwing of lots. The Bible also talks about reading the signs. And yet churches preach against divination. They're selective in what they believe and what they don't believe that's in the Bible. You can't just take pieces and preach on some without telling the whole story. This is why a lot of folks don't go to church anymore.

Look at Hosea 12:10. It tells us that God has spoken to prophets and that he has given them multiple visions and symbols so that they can be a witness:

> *I spoke to the prophets,*
> *gave them many visions*
> *and told parables through them."*

Isn't that what divination really is, being able to know things either through throwing bones, laying out the cards, or even receiving guidance through our dreams? I work with the Old Testament. That's what I was raised with. That's what I know. In the Old Testament, God gave the prophets the gift of sight so that they may go out and help the people, that they may share God's gift with the people. Men of the churches have tried to remove God's gift out of the churches, but you can't take away what God has given.

One of my favorite books in the Old Testament is the book of Isaiah. It is a powerful book, and it has a lot of Conjure work in it. If you look at Isaiah 3:2, God has put the prophets right up there with the men of war, the judges, and the elders:

> *the hero and the warrior,*
> *the judge and the prophet,*
> *the diviner and the elder,*

So do we just throw that out because a bunch of preachers are preaching that it's against God's law? No. God gave us our gifts of sight and the gift of discernment to be able to help the people just like the prophets did.

A lot of preachers will preach Deuteronomy 18:10-12 to show that God said any type of practice, witchcraft, omens, sorcery, or divination are all an abomination in God's eyes:

> *10 Let no one be found among you who sacrifices their son or daughter in the fire, who practices divination or sorcery, interprets omens, engages in witchcraft, 11 or casts spells, or who is a medium or spiritist or who consults the dead. 12 Anyone who does these things is detestable to the Lord; because of these same detestable practices the Lord your God will drive out those nations before you.*

But then if you look at Deuteronomy 18:18, we see that God is going to raise up prophets and folks who can use the skills of divination to help the people out:

> *I will raise up for them a prophet like you from among their fellow Israelites, and I will put my words in his mouth. He will tell them everything I command him.*

And in Genesis 30:27, it shows us how Laban used divination:

> *But Laban said to him, "If I have found favor in your eyes, please stay. I have learned by divination that the Lord has blessed me because of you."*

Divination is God's gift to us. It's a way for us to be able to help ourselves and others, and if you are going to do this work, you need that skill. You need to be able to know how to not only help yourself, but the folks who are going to come to you for help.

Before you do any type of work, you need to divine on it. You need to discern if you should even be doing the work at all. You have to remember that everything you do is your responsibility. The person who taught you, or the book that you read, or however you learned it, whatever action you take with that information is all your responsibility. Be wise in how you use your gifts.

I just wanted to give you some foundation on what the Bible really says about the gifts God has given us. I know some folks who get into this work come from a strong Christian background and they have been led to believe that any type of magic or divination, or prophecy, or having the gift of the sight is of the devil. I was raised to believe that it's a blessing, even though when I was young I was afraid of it. I tried to run, but I didn't get very far.

Anytime you have a skill, that skill has to be honed. You have to learn to work with the skill; it's a part of you. So if you are going to be a Conjure worker, you have to hone the skill of discernment. You have to learn to understand the messages that spirit is trying to share with you.

Throwing Bones

Animal bones have long been used to do spiritual readings. This type of reading is called bone reading. The spirit speaks to the reader through the way that the bones are laid out. When I do a bone reading for a client, I have them blow three breaths over the bones before I throw them. I do this so their spirit links with the bones. This way I get a good reading.

Reading the Cards

I don't know how to read tarot cards. I just can't. I don't know why, but I can't. But I can read playing cards, and so I want to give a little lesson that can help you out if you practice working with the cards in divination to help you find the answers you are looking for in order to help yourself and others.

You need a new deck of playing cards. You are simply going to work with these cards for divination. These cards are going to become a magical tool.

Cleansing Your Deck

The first thing that you need to do is cleanse the cards. I truly believe that all decks of cards hold a spirit. Before you ever pick up your cards, say your personal prayers and bring in protection. Here is a little prayer that you can say over your cards, or you could say your own prayer.

I call on God the father, God the son, and God the Holy Spirit. I call on all the spirits that walk with me that have my good favor in their hearts. May they fill these cards with the power of discernment in a way that I will always be able to understand. Amen.

Now take the deck out of the box, shuffle the cards three times, blow three breaths on them, lay them out on a white cloth, and cover them with table salt. You're going to leave them covered for three days.

On the fourth day, repeat your prayers and then clean the salt off of your cards. Put the salt in a white bowl and save it for later use so you can re-cleanse your cards as needed. (I have found that in the past when I've done divination for some folks my tools had to be cleansed afterward. you'll know when that time comes because your cards will feel heavy and they will stop reading true.)

Once you get all the salt off of your cards, light a white stick candle. Have a glass of water sitting next to the candle. You should always have a candle going and a glass of water when you are doing divination; the fire and the water draw in spirit.

Then shuffle your cards three times, and each time you shuffle blow a clear breath on the cards. This is done so the cards read clear. Say your prayer over your cards three times as you are shuffling, and then set your cards in front of the glass of water and the candle and let the candle burn out.

Laying Out the Cards

Every time you do a layout, you should shuffle your cards, say your prayer over the cards three times, and blow three breaths over the cards. The number three is very magical; it represents the Holy Trinity and the three nails that held Jesus on the cross, among other things.

So for this layout, to get the answer that you're looking for to see if you should even do any type of magical work on a situation, you are going to lay out three cards.

Shuffle the cards while you speak over them whatever the question may be. The first card that you draw is the foundation card: it is going to answer the question that you just posed. Assuming this card tells us to move forward, draw a second card and place it to the right. Now pull a third card and place it to the left of the center card.

Here's an example: Someone came to me for consultation wanting to know if now was the right time to open up a new business. The foundation card came out to be the Ace of Diamonds. At first glance we could say that this card is telling us to move forward because the Ace of Diamonds is a very good card; it's very positive, and it shows a strong possibility for prosperity and success. But remember, we have three cards to lay out and we've only laid one out so far, which shows us that the cards are on target because that is what the querent was asking about. Let's see what the next card is.

We drew the second card and placed it to the right. It's the Four of Spades Now this card can represent a setback. It could be a block that brings on lots of stress. So even though we got the Ace of Diamonds, which is a beautiful card and talks about success and how great everything could be, we now have the Four of Spades that's telling us, "Um, look here, things might not be as glamorous and as easy as you thought they were going to be." This card warns us that even though we may get what we're asking for, it's going to be a whole lot of mess trying to reach our goal.

Now we pull the last card. This card is placed to the left and should finish out the story. The last card is the Joker. The Joker represents the spirit and the ancestors. It also represents things that are hidden. Sometimes spirits have jokes, and I always say that when I get a layout like this one when I'm trying to figure out how to help someone. The reason I say this is because if you look at the cards that are laid out, we've got the Ace of Diamonds, which is a wonderful card; then we've got that Four of Spades, which is a warning card, basically telling us that even though it's possible, you going to have to go through so much stuff to achieve it; and then we have spirit coming in with the third card, the Joker, and saying, "I'm here with you, but you have to make the choice in the end." Layouts like this are the reason that you have to be able to discern what spirit is telling you.

In a situation like this, even though the foundation card was spot-on, I'm going to advise that the querent pray on the situation and ask for more guidance before they take that major step. I do believe that they could be successful, but I don't believe that the timing is right because that spade warns about all the stress and the blocks that are going to get in the way. Then you have spirit saying, "Hey, I'm here and I'm listening, but I'm also letting you know that it might not be as smooth sailing as you thought it was going to be."

Learning to listen to spirit takes time, and learning to understand what spirit is telling you takes time; but these are skills that you need if you are going to do this work. What would have happened if I would not have done divination on this situation and just told my client, "Yes, open a business, it's a great idea. You can do it, and it'll be successful," but then all the problems started coming in—all the stress started building up, things started going wrong before they even got started . . . That would not only make me look bad, but it would also show my client that I don't know what the heck I'm doing.

Whether you are working for yourself or someone else, you always have to do divination first to make sure that you should even be doing whatever the job might be. If you are warned not to do it, then don't do it. Spirit always knows what is best. They see everything. If you choose not to listen, then that's on you and you alone. Because at the end of every day, all day long, you and you alone are responsible for your actions and the things you do.

Using a Pendulum

Before I work with any dirts, roots, herbs, or curios, I always work my pendulum first over whatever it is that I feel like I want to add to a work. I learned a long time ago that it's better to be safe than sorry, so before you start just throwing a bunch of stuff together, make sure that it's the right stuff that you should be adding to the work that you are doing.

If you are new to working with a pendulum, then the first step would be to either make one or buy one. Making a pendulum for yourself can be as simple as tying a ring on a string; it doesn't have to be complicated. After that, you need to cleanse your pendulum under some cool running water, and then let it air dry. Like with any other tool, you will need to work with the pendulum so that it becomes a part of you and you have a bond with it. The easiest way to bond a tool is through our breath; it gives life to the tool and it also connects us to the tool we are working with.

If you are new to working with a pendulum, then you should only ask questions that you know the answers to. You need to determine what means yes and what means no. I prefer for my pendulum to move for yes and stop for no; it makes it easier to understand.

A closing note on divination. If you are wondering how to divine on each and every card, or you simply want to learn more about card layouts, bibliomancy, or the other divination methods I mention in this book, you can pick up my book *Divination Conjure Style*. In it, I do a deep dive into the meanings of every card in a standard playing deck, as well as other forms of divination.

8

Prayer

Prayer is important because it is a conversation with spirit. This is the time when you ask the spirit to intercede on your behalf, or you just tell them how grateful you are for all the blessings you have received. Prayer shouldn't be stressful or something you feel you have to do! It should be a peaceful time when you can interact with spirit. I know that some folks might not know how to pray or where to even start. It's really simple: you start from the heart. You can pour your heart out and receive the answer you are looking for.

If you are not sure how to pray, this may help. Find a quiet place where you can sit and be still. This can be at the beach, on a park bench, or even at the kitchen table. Settle your mind and get yourself settled, then just start speaking the words from your heart. Just let it all pour out. Spirit will hear you and they will answer you. We have to remember, though, like the old folks say, "our time ain't God's time." We have to be patient for spirit to answer. The more you get into the habit of praying, the easier it will become. Just relax and don't overthink it.

Working with the Bible

Conjure is not a religion, per say, but most old-school workers are Christian, and the Bible is a powerful tool in the work. I don't believe when the ancestors were brought over here on the slave ships that they were Christians. History and old stories tell us that they were forced into

Christianity. Instead of them being made to bend to Christianity, they made Christianity their own. They made the Bible work for them.

I have dealt with a lot of clients in the years I have been working for the public. The one thing that always comes up when I am giving them instructions on what I need for them to do as their part of the work is prayer and petition. They're the same thing; a prayer is a petition to spirit to help.

Here is the petition I work with. This is for crossed conditions. When things start going wrong in your life and it continues on for a long time, that could be a crossed condition. A crossed condition is when someone has done spiritual work on you. It's like a jinx, or what in witchcraft is called a curse.

God's Petition

I Petition Thee, God on high and the almighty spirits that walk with you, Lord. I come to you in prayer and petition that you will remove all crossed conditions that may be affecting my life. Remove them with your mighty hand. I ask this in the name of God the Father, God the Son, and the God the Holy Spirit. Amen.

I Petition the Holy Trinity. Please remove all blocks and crossed conditions that may be affecting me and mine. I ask this in the name of God the Father, God the Son, and God the Holy Spirit. Amen.

I petition Thee, St. Michael, God's right-hand man, sever all ties to all my enemies known, unknown, hidden, alive, and dead that work against me day and night, dark and light. Destroy all crossed conditions that bind my spirit. With your mighty Sword cut all ties to all my enemies! Amen.

I Pray that the Holy Trinity will protect me and shield me against all my enemies. I pray for the gift of Discernment so I may know them by the darkness of their spirit. I pray the Trinity will gift me with the Spirit of Truth and Wisdom so that I may always see what is hidden and done in the dark so it may be brought to light. I pray this in the name of God the Father, God the Son, and God the Holy Spirit, and in the name of the Ancestors. Amen.

I call on my Ancestors, Known and Unknown, blood of my blood, and all the spirits that walk with me. I ask that you protect and defend me against all those who would harm me or mine. I pray that every hit be returned tenfold in the name of God the Father, God the Son, and God the Holy Spirit, and the Ancestors and all the spirits that walk with me. Amen.

I cover this prayer and my petition with the blood of Jesus! I cover my enemies and any works they have laid against me with the blood of Jesus; may it burn and be destroyed! I call on the Holy Trinity to guard me and keep me and mine safe! Amen.

You can work with that petition and at the end of it pray for whatever your need might be. If you are praying the petition for someone else, then after each verse you need to call out their name and pray the prayer for whatever they need. The same goes for the Bible verse. If you are praying over someone, then you need to add their name to the Bible verse.

There are all types of works in the Bible to help with everyday life; you can find works for love, a peaceful home, justice, and even enemy work. I'm going to share a few of these works here so you get the idea of how to do the work. But first a reminder: The Bible is not all love and light, and neither is Conjure work. You are responsible for the works you do and the prayers you pray.

Enemy Work

We're going to look at a few different verses in the Bible that deal with enemy work. I'm going to try to explain how to do the work in an easy manner. The one thing that you have to remember is that all works that you do should be justified. Some of the works can be very harsh, but as long as the work is justified then you are safe in doing it. If you do unjustified works, then you are taking the chance of getting hit with your own work if the target is well-versed in the work and does a reversal or cleansing.

The first one we're going to look at is Romans 12:20:

On the contrary:
"If your enemy is hungry, feed him;
*   if he is thirsty, give him something to drink.*
In doing this, you will heap burning coals on his head."

As you can see, the instructions in this verse say that if your enemy is hungry, feed him. If he is thirsty, give him something to drink. In doing this, you are the righteous one. You are not the one who is doing something wrong. You've done everything right. Then God says, basically, when you do the right thing and you are not in the wrong that he will heap burning coals on your enemy's head. So when you work this, you can literally turn this on your enemy. At the end of the verse you would say your petition, something like,

"Lord, you know who my enemies are. You know that my
heart is pure. You know that I've done nothing wrong to
them. Set them down that they may not lift a hand to me or
mine. Your word says that you would heap burning coals on
their heads. Protect me and mine. Amen!"

Micah 5:9 is another good source to counter an enemy's influence:

Your hand will be lifted up in triumph over your enemies,
*   and all your foes will be destroyed.*

You could say a petition like this one:

"Lord, your word says that your hand will be lifted up
against my enemies, that all my foes will be destroyed; cut
them down so that I may live in peace and happiness! Amen."

You can light a red vigil or red stick candle while you pray this petition. It is better not to call names of a target when doing this type of work because you don't know what the enemy looks like. Sometimes it's folks we think are in our corner. Spirit always knows, so trust them to know who is who.

Protection

Light a white or red candle and pray Ephesians 6:11-17 over the candle:

> 11 Put on the full armor of God, so that you can take your stand against the devil's schemes. 12 For our struggle is not against flesh and blood, but against the rulers, against the authorities, against the powers of this dark world and against the spiritual forces of evil in the heavenly realms. 13 Therefore put on the full armor of God, so that when the day of evil comes, you may be able to stand your ground, and after you have done everything, to stand. 14 Stand firm then, with the belt of truth buckled around your waist, with the breastplate of righteousness in place, 15 and with your feet fitted with the readiness that comes from the gospel of peace. 16 In addition to all this, take up the shield of faith, with which you can extinguish all the flaming arrows of the evil one. 17 Take the helmet of salvation and the sword of the Spirit, which is the word of God.

If you are praying this for someone else, then you call their name after each verse. I would do this for nine days.

Shut Your Mouth

Gossip can be a killer; some folks love to run their mouths, and they don't care who it hurts or the lives it can destroy. I used to try to understand folks who couldn't mind their own business and who were always running their mouths about other people. I have come to the conclusion that these types of folks don't have any control over their own lives and they don't have any peace, and so their way of getting excitement and attention is to run their mouth and stick their nose in other folks' business. These types of folks love drama, they love stirring the pot and keeping things going all the time.

So if you find yourself in a situation where you need to defend yourself against gossip, light a white candle (I prefer a stick candle when I'm doing this type of work) and pray Isaiah 54:17:

> *"No weapon forged against you will prevail,*
>> *and you will refute every tongue that accuses you.*
> *This is the heritage of the servants of the LORD,*
>> *and this is their vindication from me,"*
> *declares the LORD.*

Then pray,

> *"Lord, you said that every tongue that shall rise up against me shall be condemned; I petition you, Lord, to shut those tongues that they may never rise up against me again! Amen."*

I would do this work for at least nine days.

Peaceful Home

We all deserve to have peace in our homes but there are times when it seems like our home has become a battlefield. When there's arguing, fighting, and upset going on, these are the times when a peaceful home spiritual work is needed. Spiritually cleansing the home includes washing the inside and outside of the doors. You should also sweep in the corners of the rooms. My mama believed that upset within the home would hide in the corners just waiting to get stirred up again.

Lavender is great for peaceful home works because of its soothing nature. A simple wash of lavender, basil, and four tablespoons of salt can be used to cleanse the home. Make the wash and pray Leviticus 26 verse 6 over it, then add the salt to the wash. That should bring about peace.

Leviticus 26:6

*"'I will grant peace in the land, and you will lie down and
no one will make you afraid. I will remove wild beasts from
the land, and the sword will not pass through your country.*

Salt holds a memory. If you only had salt to use, you could pray the
verse over the salt and then use the wash to cleanse the doors and the
area where the upset is happening. Use what you have! Prayer in itself
is a powerful tool.

The broom is also a great tool to move upset out of the home and
to bring peace. You can pray Leviticus 26:6 over the head of the broom
and use the broom to sweep the furniture, walls, and floors while praying that peace rains down on the home. Simply sweep the troubles out
of the door.

9

Offerings

I have touched on offerings before in my writing but I have never really gone into detail. I felt like, with this book, because I wanted to help both the novice and the experienced workers, it was important to more deeply cover offerings, because a novice might not know much about offerings. For me, offerings are very important because I don't want to work for nothing, so I believe that spirit in turn doesn't want to always be called on and petitioned for things without getting anything in return. My motto is and always has been, "No one works for nothing." Everyone deserves to get paid in one way or another for the things they do. Spirit is no different. If you call in on me all the time and you want help and you need this and you need that and I'm not getting anything in return, then after a while I'm going to stop answering the call. I truly believe that spirit feels the same way.

I'm not sure if they expect it or not, but we should always show our gratitude for the blessings that we have received. Yes, we put in the work, put in our time; but at the end of every day spirit is the one that gives us our blessings. I don't care what kind of God or what kind of spirits you worship or honor—that's not my business, that's between you and your god—but you really need to learn to show your appreciation for what spirit has given you, and one way to do this is through an offering. An offering can be something as simple as a cool glass of water if that's all you have to offer. Nobody's saying that you have to break the bank, but you should always be fair with your offerings because spirit is fair with you.

What Is an Appropriate Offering?

There are many different types of offerings that can be given to spirit. They vary from fruits and vegetables to whole plates of food. This is what most folks offer. But if you were taught how to work with the Old Testament, then you know that there are many other types of offerings. Some of these offerings are meat offerings, some are burnt offerings. There are many different reasons why these things would be offered.

The offerings should be left for at least three days on the altar, then they should be taken and left in the woods. These offerings are like any other offerings you give to spirit: You should always honor the spirits with a personal prayer. Speak to them from the heart.

What the Bible Says about Offerings

The Bible plays a big part in Conjure work—especially the Old Testament. Some workers choose not to work with the Bible, but that's on them. I'm writing about what I know , where I live, and what I've been taught. The Bible is full of information that goes with this work if you know where to find it.

I have never in my life been one to follow someone blindly. I want to know—I want you to show me—where the information is, how you found out about it, and then I'll put that information to work for myself and my people. If you look in the Bible, there are a couple different types of offerings. The burnt offering was where animals were slaughtered, and the meat was offered up as an offering. Then there is the grain offering. This is where grain was offered, and it was heavily salted. The Bible also talks about a peace offering. This was a gathering of friends and family in order to draw peace among the people. And there is a purification offering, which we know is for cleansings and purifying the spirit.

Now, we're living in the 21st Century, not in the days of the Bible, so some things are going to change. Sometimes things have to change in order to meet the times that you're living in. Working with the Bible is no different. It is impossible to follow the Old Testament word for word—you might end up in jail. The work has to adjust to modern times, but the foundation of the work shouldn't be changed. If you look in Leviticus 1-7, for example, they explain the offerings and the old way of making the offerings. Nowadays you can offer animal parts from the butcher or the grocery store and the offering will be received just as well.

When you're looking in the Old Testament and it's talking about offerings, some verses suggest that you do an offering every day. Others suggest you do them on special occasions. In this busy world that we live in, if you could do an offering once a week just to show how grateful you are for the blessings that you've been given, I think it would be enough. As we will see, it often can be as simple as a bowl of salt or as elaborate as you want it to be. The important thing is that you are showing your appreciation to spirit for the blessings you are being blessed with.

In Leviticus 6 verse 12, you will find instructions for keeping a fire always going on your altar and not letting it go out:

> The fire on the altar must be kept burning; it must not
> go out. Every morning the priest is to add firewood and
> arrange the burnt offering on the fire and burn the fat of
> the fellowship offerings on it.

In this instance, they are talking about oil lamps that were made with a cotton wick. We have to remember that back in the day, the fat from animals was used to make candles and lamps. But if you don't know how to make a lamp and you want to keep a fire going on your altar, you could just burn a candle.

Burnt Offering

Leviticus 1 verses 14-17 explains how to make a burnt offering of a bird:

> 14 "If the offering to the Lord is a burnt offering of birds,
> you are to offer a dove or a young pigeon. 15 The priest shall
> bring it to the altar, wring off the head and burn it on the

altar; its blood shall be drained out on the side of the altar.
16 He is to remove the crop and the feathers[a] and throw
them down east of the altar where the ashes are. 17 He shall
tear it open by the wings, not dividing it completely, and
then the priest shall burn it on the wood that is burning on
the altar. It is a burnt offering, a food offering, an aroma
pleasing to the Lord.

I need to make this clear: *I'm speaking of old-school Conjure,*
nothing more. Nowadays, you can buy a bird already dressed from the
butcher or the grocery store, so there is no reason to kill an animal to
give an offering.

Grain Offering

In Leviticus 2:1, God gives us the instructions on the offering:

"'When anyone brings a grain offering to the Lord, their
offering is to be of the finest flour. They are to pour olive
oil on it, put incense on it

You can offer a cup of fine flour that you have poured a little olive
oil over, and put some frankincense on top of it. To this I would add a
white stick candle in the center of the offering. That would be perfect
for a weekly offering.

Leviticus 6:14–17 contains clear instructions for the grain offering:

14 "'These are the regulations for the grain offering: Aar-
on's sons are to bring it before the Lord, in front of the altar.
15 The priest is to take a handful of the finest flour and
some olive oil, together with all the incense on the grain
offering, and burn the memorial portion on the altar as an
aroma pleasing to the Lord. 16 Aaron and his sons shall eat
the rest of it, but it is to be eaten without yeast in the sanc-
tuary area; they are to eat it in the courtyard of the tent of
meeting. 17 It must not be baked with yeast; I have given it
as their share of the food offerings presented to me. Like the
sin offering and the guilt offering, it is most holy.

It goes on and speaks a little more in verses 21-23:

21 It must be prepared with oil on a griddle; bring it well-mixed and present the grain offering broken in pieces as an aroma pleasing to the Lord. 22 The son who is to succeed him as anointed priest shall prepare it. It is the Lord's perpetual share and is to be burned completely. 23 Every grain offering of a priest shall be burned completely; it must not be eaten."

There has always been a debate on whether to give spirit salted or unsalted food. If you look at Leviticus 2:13, it says that the offering of the grain should be well salted and that salt should not be lacking from the offering. It also says that salt should be offered with every offering you give:

Season all your grain offerings with salt. Do not leave the salt of the covenant of your God out of your grain offerings; add salt to all your offerings.

Salt not only purifies, but it also can hold prayers and petitions, so anything that is added to it spiritually will hold the prayers and petitions that are prayed over that offering. So if you only had salt to give, that would make a good offering. I believe that spirit will accept whatever you have to give. If all you have is a spoon of grits, offer it.

If you look at Numbers 28:8, you can see that there is an offering of grain, something to drink, and an offer made by fire that's delicious-smelling:

Offer the second lamb at twilight, along with the same kind of grain offering and drink offering that you offer in the morning. This is a food offering, an aroma pleasing to the LORD.

So a simple offering could be a bowl of rice or oatmeal with a stick candle stuck in it and burned. (Of course, you have to be smart when you're messing with fire and make sure that it's in a fire-resistant container.) That would make a great offering.

Peace Offering

The offering described in Leviticus 3 can be given for peace in the home and also for peace in your life. You can find animal kidneys at the butcher.

Leviticus 3:3-6

3 From the fellowship offering you are to bring a food offering to the Lord: the internal organs and all the fat that is connected to them, 4 both kidneys with the fat on them near the loins, and the long lobe of the liver, which you will remove with the kidneys. 5 Then Aaron's sons are to burn it on the altar on top of the burnt offering that is lying on the burning wood; it is a food offering, an aroma pleasing to the Lord.

6 "If you offer an animal from the flock as a fellowship offering to the Lord, you are to offer a male or female without defect.

Sin Offering

A sin offering is an offering made to absolve yourself of sin.

Leviticus 5:4, 11-13:

4 or if anyone thoughtlessly takes an oath to do anything, whether good or evil (in any matter one might carelessly swear about) even though they are unaware of it, but then they learn of it and realize their guilt—

11 "If, however, they cannot afford two doves or two young pigeons, they are to bring as an offering for their sin a tenth of an ephah [about 3.5 pounds] of the finest flour for a sin offering. They must not put olive oil or incense on it, because it is a sin offering. 12 They are to bring it to the priest, who shall take a handful of it as a memorial portion and burn it on the altar on top of the food offerings presented to the Lord. It is a sin offering. 13 In this way the priest will make atonement for them for any of these sins they have committed, and they will be forgiven. The rest of the offering will belong to the priest, as in the case of the grain offering.'"

Trespass Offering

A trespass offering, like a sin offering, is an offering given so that a transgression is forgiven. Back in that time, it seems a lot of things were sins or trespasses.

Leviticus 5:14-19

14 The Lord said to Moses: 15 "When anyone is unfaithful to the Lord by sinning unintentionally in regard to any of the Lord's holy things, they are to bring to the Lord as a penalty a ram from the flock, one without defect and of the proper value in silver, according to the sanctuary shekel. It is a guilt offering. 16 They must make restitution for what they have failed to do in regard to the holy things, pay an additional penalty of a fifth of its value and give it all to the priest. The priest will make atonement for them with the ram as a guilt offering, and they will be forgiven.

17 "If anyone sins and does what is forbidden in any of the Lord's commands, even though they do not know it, they are guilty and will be held responsible. 18 They are to bring to the priest as a guilt offering a ram from the flock, one without defect and of the proper value. In this way the priest will make atonement for them for the wrong they have committed unintentionally, and they will be forgiven. 19 It is a guilt offering; they have been guilty of wrongdoing against the Lord."

One thing I know for sure after doing this work all these years is that if you are good to your spirits, they will be good to you. And I know that in this day and age everybody is busy working taking care of their families, doing all the things that we have to do in everyday life—but you have to make time for the spirits that walk with you, that take care of you, that are always there for you. In the long run you will be blessed beyond measure for taking care of them.

10

The Arms of the Cross

To the Conjure worker, the cross is more than just a religious symbol—it is a thing of power. When you are working with the cross, it is a way to draw something to you, to dominate, to nail down, and the cross also can be worked with for healing and cleansing. It can represent the four corners, or directions: north, south, east, and west.

I have a couple of different flat wooden crosses I work with. I don't work with the same cross for positive works that I work with for negative works. I don't mix the different energies. You can even work with a paper cross if you don't have a wooden one. Conjure is all about working with what you have.

It is very important that you understand how to work with the cross in the right way, otherwise you could cause yourself harm. This is one of the reasons it is important to find an elder or a teacher to teach you how to do this work. I know the work seems simple, but don't let that fool you. This work can be dangerous, and you could cause yourself issues. For example, if you went left to right on something that you were trying to draw to you, you would be nailing it down; it wouldn't ever come to you. You could cause yourself more harm than good. It has taken me fifty-plus years to learn what I know, and I still don't know everything. Just take it slow, pay attention to what you are doing, and don't be afraid to ask for help.

When you are working with the cross, it's important that you understand the way you lay your tools down upon the cross. If you are trying to open something up, then you would lay your candles out on top of the cross, top to bottom, then right to left. If you are trying to nail something or someone down, you would lay the candles out top to bottom, then left to right. If you notice, you crossed over across the arms of the cross. When you cross over the arms of the cross, you are nailing down whatever you are working on. If you are doing prosperity work, job work, healing work, or any of those types of work, you would not go from left to right, because if you did you would be holding yourself in place. So if you didn't have any money, you'd be stuck there. If you were looking for a job, you'd never find a job—you just nailed yourself down to be unemployed. If you were ill, you just nailed that sickness down on yourself.

I want to give four works, one for each arm of the cross, to give you an idea of how to work with each arm. North is earth, fire is in the south, air is in the east, and water is in the west.

If you look at the arms of the cross, the top would be the north and the earth. The dead are buried in the earth, and nothing grows in the north. The bottom arm of the cross is the south, and we know that fire sits in the south. Next is the east, which is the right-hand arm of the cross. The sun rises in the east. This part of the cross is worked with to draw things to you. The left side of the cross, which would be the left arm, belongs to the west. The sun sets in the west, so that side of the cross would be worked with to remove things or move things away from you.

I'm what folks call a two-headed worker, which means that I will do what folks call "light" or "dark" work just as long as the work is justified. This is why there has to be some type of divination done on the work before it's started; you use divination to get confirmation on whether the work is justified.

I just want to say this again before I go any further: You and you alone are responsible for the works you do. Make sure that all works are justified. That way, if a reversal or some other type of work is done by the target, they will be wasting their time because it will not touch you. Another thing is that just because you know how to do something doesn't mean you have to do it. So take responsibility for your own actions. And remember that every action causes a reaction!

The North

I'm going to start with the top of the cross, the north/earth. The north for me is kind of a contradiction, because earth is in the north and we know that things grow in the earth. And yet, most of the time, when things are planted in the north they grow very slowly, or they might not grow at all. I know this from experience—we planted some shrubbery on the north side of our house and it has taken that shrubbery years to reach the height of our fence.

In Conjure, the north is worked with when you want to slow something or someone down. If you had a target you needed to hold down, then working the top of the cross is the way to do the work. Because the north is a place where things move slowly, you could also bury a work or a photo of the target in the north.

This work is used to keep someone locked up in jail. Please remember to make sure the work is justified before you do the work. This is not a sweet, sugary work; so once again, if you feel uncomfortable with a work, don't do it.

To start, you will need to gather these things: a photo of the target, three nails, some dirt from the north side of a jail, twenty-one small white stick candles, and a box of some kind. (The box doesn't have to have a lid on it because you are not going to bury the box.)

Cut the photo into the shape of a cross. Put the dirt from the north side of a jail in the box. Lay the cross, aka the target, on top of the dirt in the box. Then take one of the nails and stick it in the left side of the cross and say, "I nail you down with the nail that nailed Jesus's left hand to the cross." Then nail down the right side of the cross and say, "I nail you down with the nail that nailed Jesus's right hand to the cross." You then nail down the bottom of the cross and say, "I nail you down with the nail that nailed Jesus's feet to the cross." Then you cover the cross up with more dirt until you can't see the cross at all.

Light one candle a day for twenty-one days. Once the candle is lit, say your petition and prayer over the work. After the twenty-one days, put the work up in a safe place. Then, once a month, take it out and work it for three days. If you decide to set the target free, burn the cross and blow the ashes into the east.

The South

We're moving to the bottom of the cross, which is the south. The south is warm, and it is worked with to bring warmth into a relationship, love into a home, or for things that need to be heated up. The south is where we find fire. As we all know, fire burns hot. It can lend its power to a work or it can also destroy a target.

To Heat a Work Up

One way to work with the bottom of the cross is to place a work that you are doing with intent to heat the work up. For example, if you are trying to get a loan from a bank and the bank is dragging their feet getting the loan done, you could place the cross on top of a copy of the loan application. Then set a red candle on top of the bottom arm of the cross. Pray your personal petition to the spirit of the cross to get the loan pushed through. You would say your prayer and petition at least three times a day, calling out the bank's name, the loan officer's name, and the amount of money that you are trying to borrow from the bank. Remember that a personal petition is one that comes from the heart of the person who is petitioning spirit for help. Speak from the heart.

To Destroy an Enemy

This work is not all sugary and sweet. You have to remember that this work was borne out of a time when one person could own another, when families were torn apart for a dollar. A time when an owner could kill another person for looking them in the eye! This work is borne out of slavery, so it is not going to be all sweet. The ancestors did what they had to do to live.

The knowledge of these old works is being lost as the elders are dying. I know some folks think I give away too many "secrets," but it's important to me that this work live on. There is already too much mixing and moxing of the work being done; it's being whitewashed and sugared. (When I say whitewashed, I am not talking about white people! When I was growing up, folks would add water to the white paint to make it stretch, which in turn watered the paint down.) If a work doesn't sit with your spirit, move around and don't do that work, plain and simple.

We have to remember that where there is light there is also darkness. Nothing is ever one-sided. The same goes for this work. You are the only one who can decide how far you are willing to go. For me, if the work is justified, then I'm going to do it!

The next work is a serious work and shouldn't be done just because someone made you mad. Always remember, every action causes a reaction. If you go after a target unjustly, spirit will step in. I'm a firm believer that spirit sees all and knows all; they know what we don't and see what we can't see. So I'm going to give you a little sage advice: If you decide to do this next work, don't call out a target's name. Let spirit do the justice for you.

This work is placed on the south end, or bottom of the cross. On a paper write, "all my enemies known and unknown." Place the paper under the cross. Place a white stick candle on the foot of the cross and light it. I'm going to give you a couple of different verses I have prayed over the years with this work. Pick the chapter and verse that feels right to you and sits well with your spirit.

Isaiah 29:6

the Lord Almighty will come
with thunder and earthquake and great noise,
with windstorm and tempest and flames of a devouring fire.

Ezekiel 28:18

By your many sins and dishonest trade
you have desecrated your sanctuaries.
So I made a fire come out from you,
and it consumed you,
and I reduced you to ashes on the ground
in the sight of all who were watching.

Isaiah 34:9

[Her] streams will be turned into pitch,
her dust into burning sulfur;
her land will become blazing pitch!

Revelation 11:5

If anyone tries to harm them, fire comes from their mouths and devours their enemies. This is how anyone who wants to harm them must die.

At the end of each verse, petition that all your enemies be destroyed. Say the prayer three times a day over the cross. Let each stick candle burn completely out.

The East

The next arm we are going to look at is the right side, or the east. The sun rises in the east every morning. Since it rises, it draws things that we need to us. I was taught that anything I wanted to be brought to me should be worked in the east. If there is something you are trying to bring into your life, or for all positive works, you place it on the right arm of the cross.

Here's an example. About twenty years ago, we were trying to buy a prime piece of land. The lady kept going back and forth with selling the land. So I got some of the dirt off the land and placed it on the cross. I worked that dirt, and finally when she was ready to sell, she sold to us.

When doing this type of work dealing with land or a big, costly item, I always throw into my petition, "if it is right for me." Sometimes we feel we need or want something, and it is not the right thing for us. It is better to place it in spirit's hands than force the work. That's how I look at it.

If you are trying to draw something to you, you can either work with a petition or a photo. Place it on the right arm of the cross. Burn a candle for three to twenty-one days on the work. Then burn the work to ash and blow the ashes into the east to finish the work. Here are some Bible verses you can work with:

Luke 6:38

Give, and it will be given to you. A good measure, pressed down, shaken together and running over, will be poured into your lap. For with the measure you use, it will be measured to you."

Malachi 3:10

Bring the whole tithe into the storehouse, that there may be food in my house. Test me in this," says the Lord Almighty, "and see if I will not throw open the floodgates of heaven and pour out so much blessing that there will not be room enough to store it.

Ephesians 3:20

Now to him who is able to do immeasurably more than all we ask or imagine, according to his power that is at work within us,

The best time to do this work is when the sun is high in the sky, or what the old folks call high noon. That's because the east is the place where the sun rises, and high noon is the time it is believed that the power is high and at its peak.

The West

The last arm of the cross is the left arm, which is in the west. The west is the place where the sun goes down to rest every day. As a Conjure worker, I have been taught that anything I need to remove from my life is put into the west. As we know, the sun goes down in the west and brings forth darkness, so working in the west is good for a multitude of things. I was taught when doing this type of work that the best time to lay something or someone to rest is when the afternoon sun is high in the sky, right before it starts to go down for the night.

Just like when you are working in the east, you can burn things and blow them into the west to remove them. If you have a situation or a target that needs to be removed from your life, you can take one of the Bible verses below and write the petition over it.

Zephaniah 3:15

The Lord has taken away your punishment,
*   he has turned back your enemy.*
The Lord, the King of Israel, is with you;
*   never a gain will you fear any harm.*

Isaiah 62:8

The Lord has sworn by his right hand
   and by his mighty arm:
"Never again will I give your grain
   as food for your enemies,
and never again will foreigners drink the new wine
   for which you have toiled;

2 Samuel 22:18

He rescued me from my powerful enemy,
   from my foes, who were too strong for me.

Place the petition on the left arm of the cross. Every day, when the afternoon sun is at its highest before it starts to go down, light a candle on top of the petition and say your prayer for whatever it is you need removed. Do this at least three days in a row. On the fourth day, burn the petition and blow it into the west just when the sun starts to set.

PART III

Symbols and Signs

In our house growing up, signs were a big thing. My mama didn't say, "This means this"—we learned by listening to her. If she saw a bunch of cattle laid up together, she would always say, "A storm is coming, be it inside the house or outside." Now when I see them laid up, my mind automatically knows something is coming, I heard it so much as a kid. This is how kids are taught when a family is living Conjure, and not just doing the work when they need something.

I grew up on the signs. If I see cows huddled in a field, I know either a storm is coming or the weather is fixing to change. If the broom falls in my home, I know company is coming to visit. A rooster crowing after midnight means a big change is coming to the home. Roosters are usually in their roost sleeping at that time and they are very sensitive to the change around them. Animals can sense and see spirits. Estella, my Yorkie, is very sensitive to them and when she feels one that might not be all love and light, she starts a low growl and will just sit in one spot looking. I know when she does that that there is something there and she is warning me about it.

Anytime I pass by a group of buzzards on the side of the road, I know I need to do some cleansing work and offer an offering. I can't tell you how I know. It's something that's ingrained in me from when I was a child. The thing with the buzzard is that it will eat anything down to the bone, so for me they are a sign that I am missing something and it needs to be taken care of. Is this all superstition or folk tales? I don't know for sure, but I am not testing the waters of the way I was raised. I guess for folks who didn't grow up like this, it may seem strange, but for me and mine, it's a normal way of life. Learning to recognize signs can be a very powerful thing.

11

Numbers in Conjure

Numbers are important in most spiritual modalities. (Thank you, Aunt Sindy Todo, for the new word I learned from you.) They can represent many different things, and Conjure is no different. Numbers hold power and can give extra insight when we are looking for answers. Have you ever wondered why a worker will give you a certain number of baths to do or have you pray a certain amount of times? Believe it or not, the Bible is full of numbers, what they mean and the signs they show us. I'm not going to go into great detail here, but I did want to show you a little and explain how I was taught. The Bible is a powerful book and holds a lot of secrets. Folks overlook them because Christianity has left such a sour taste in a lot of folks' mouths, but we should never throw out the baby with the bathwater!

The Bible tells us a lot when we look at the days and the number of things that happen back in those days. You simply have to know what you are looking for and how to find it.

1

One is for God and all things holy. Sometimes one cleansing or one work is all you need to do.

3

The number three is one of those power numbers that is important to Conjure, as I was taught by my elders. Three represents the Holy Trinity: God the Father, God the Son, and God the Holy Spirit. The old folks believe that bad luck runs its course in threes, as does death in a family. If you look deeper in the Bible, it tells us that when God speaks you will hear it three times. The crow crowed three times with St. Peter and each time St. Peter denied Jesus. Jesus rose up on the third day. As a young worker, my elders taught me to pray over my work three times.

4

Did you know that four in the Hebrew language means "door"? In Conjure the number four represents the crossroads. If you look in Revelations 7:1-3 you will see that God sent four angels to the four corners of the earth. Four also represents the four elements: earth, air, fire, and water. It also represents the four directions, which are very important in Conjure work. We went into great detail on the four directions in the last chapter, "The Arms of the Cross."

I also want to touch on the four corners of the house. When you do protection work on your home, you should always add the four corners of your home to the work. You can do this by dressing the four corners of the home, or burying something at each of the corners of the home. There are many different ways to do this, but when you are doing protection work on your home, do not forget those four corners.

5

The number five in Conjure represents the crossroads, with the spirits in the center. It can also represent the parts of the body: we have five fingers on each hand and five toes on each foot, and we were gifted the five senses. If you remember, Jesus fed the multitude with five loaves of bread when he turned water into wine. The number five also conveys the five books where God's laws can be found: Genesis, Exodus, Leviticus, Numbers, and Deuteronomy.

When we look deeper and understand what we are looking at, the number five is a very powerful number. Remember, Jesus had five wounds inflicted on his body before he died: there were two on his feet, one on each hand, and the crown on his head. These are the same places that are worked with to nail a target down.

Leviticus 1:13-17 says that there are five animals that may be offered as a burnt sacrifice.

3 "'If the offering is a burnt offering from the herd, you are to offer a male without defect. You must present it at the entrance to the tent of meeting so that it will be acceptable to the Lord. 4 You are to lay your hand on the head of the burnt offering, and it will be accepted on your behalf to make atonement for you. 5 You are to slaughter the young bull before the Lord, and then Aaron's sons the priests shall bring the blood and splash it against the sides of the altar at the entrance to the tent of meeting. 6 You are to skin the burnt offering and cut it into pieces. 7 The sons of Aaron the priest are to put fire on the altar and arrange wood on the fire. 8 Then Aaron's sons the priests shall arrange the pieces, including the head and the fat, on the wood that is burning on the altar. 9 You are to wash the internal organs and the legs with water, and the priest is to burn all of it on the altar. It is a burnt offering, a food offering, an aroma pleasing to the Lord.

10 "'If the offering is a burnt offering from the flock, from either the sheep or the goats, you are to offer a male without defect. 11 You are to slaughter it at the north side of the altar before the Lord, and Aaron's sons the priests shall splash its blood against the sides of the altar. 12 You are to cut it into pieces, and the priest shall arrange them, including the head and the fat, on the wood that is burning on the altar. 13 You are to wash the internal organs and the legs with water, and the priest is to bring all of them and burn them on the altar. It is a burnt offering, a food offering, an aroma pleasing to the Lord.

14 "If the offering to the Lord is a burnt offering of birds, you are to offer a dove or a young pigeon. 15 The priest shall bring it to the altar, wring off the head and burn it on the altar; its blood shall be drained out on the side of the altar. 16 He is to remove the crop and the feathers[a] and throw them down east of the altar where the ashes are. 17 He shall tear it open by the wings, not dividing it completely, and then the priest shall burn it on the wood that is burning on the altar. It is a burnt offering, a food offering, an aroma pleasing to the Lord.

7

The number seven is a number of completion, meaning it's the number that represents being done with a job or an issue. God created the world in six days. On the seventh day, he rested. He was through with his job. God blessed us with seven great bodies of water and the seven colors of the rainbow.

9

Nine is worked with when you want to nail something down. If we look at 1 Corinthians 12 ,we see that God has gifted nine gifts to the people: wisdom, knowledge, faith, healing, miracles, prophecy, discernment, speaking in tongues, and the interpretation of tongues.

7 Now to each one the manifestation of the Spirit is given for the common good. 8 To one there is given through the Spirit a message of wisdom, to another a message of knowledge by means of the same Spirit, 9 to another faith by the same Spirit, to another gifts of healing by that one Spirit, 10 to another miraculous powers, to another prophecy, to another distinguishing between spirits, to another speaking in different kinds of tongues, and to still another the interpretation of tongues. 11 All these are the work of one and the same Spirit, and he distributes them to each one, just as he determines.

21

Twenty-one is for those hard cases when you are weighted down and can't get relief. Some elders have taught me that twenty-one is a very powerful number because if you add 2 + 1 it equals three, which is the Holy Trinity. When I make my products, I work on them for twenty-one days. If I feel like I have a strong resistance going on in my life, I will do three different works for seven days each, for a total of twenty-one days.

There are many aspects to Conjure work. It's more than just putting a bunch of roots and herbs together and doing the work. I wanted to share this information with you to give you an idea of how the number of ingredients you work with in a specific work plays a part in your success.

I also wanted to give these examples because I have never followed anyone blindly, and I don't expect my readers to follow me blindly. I wanted to show you where the information comes from, why the elders worked with this information and taught their students to work with this information.

I know a lot of preachers preach against divination and numerology and all of these things, but as you can see, it comes straight out of the Bible. Numerology is a big thing in the Bible, and I hope I have shown y'all some good information that you can grow and learn from.

12

Animals in Conjure

Animals are a very important part of Conjure work. They have been since the beginning. They are watched for signs to see how they act to tell what is going on. When you are working with any animal in Conjure, you need to have knowledge of that animal. You need to know the animal's traits, how they move, what they do, where they live, and so on. This will tell you how you can work with that animal's spirit. Always be respectful and mindful of what you are doing when you are working with any animal spirit.

Sometimes animal body parts are worked with in Conjure—organs, bones, feathers, pelts. In olden times, animals were sacrificed to the gods for their favor. I know some old Conjure workers might sacrifice a rooster or newborn chick when they had a job to do that didn't seem to be going anywhere. But from what I have been taught, sacrifice is *not* normally done in Conjure. Nowadays, we use meat or organs from a butcher for our work.

In this section, I want to talk about learning to read animals but also how to work with their organs in Conjure. Parts of the body can be worked with for healings, love works, domination, controlling, the list just goes on. This is a practice that is being lost with this new age of Conjure work.

Even the Bible talks about animals and how they can teach us their wisdom. In Job 12:7-9, the Bible tells us to speak to the birds in the sky and they will teach us; to speak to the earth, and the earth will teach us;

or to go to the sea and talk to the fish and they will give us the information we are seeking:

> 7 *"But ask the animals, and they will teach you,*
>   *or the birds in the sky, and they will tell you;*
>
> 8 *or speak to the earth, and it will teach you,*
>   *or let the fish in the sea inform you.*
>
> 9 *Which of all these does not know*
>   *that the hand of the* LORD *has done this?*

The Bible is a powerful book that is filled with knowledge and wisdom if you know where to look for it.

Birds

In Leviticus 11:13-19, the Bible lists which birds we cannot eat, including eagles, vultures, kites, owls, hawks, bats, and more.

Old folks say that the feathers of birds also bring messages when you find them—especially those from a raven or a crow.

Bats

In Conjure work, the bat is worked with to see what is hidden in the dark. The bat has very good eyesight at night, so they are good at showing things that are hidden in the dark—works and such that folks think can't be found.

Blue Birds

The blue bird is said to bring messages from the ancestors. It is also said that if you see one, the spirits are trying to contact you. They bring forth healings and blessings. It is very lucky to find one of their feathers. They are also looked at as a sign that your goal is almost met; you just need to keep pushing to reach total success.

Chickens

For as long as I can remember, I have been attracted to roosters and chickens. Both hens and roosters are important in Conjure.

HENS

Hens are very powerful. A fresh hen egg is the best type of egg to work with when you are doing spiritual cleansings. The egg is also good for protection. Spirit cannot tell the difference between a human or an egg because they are both live things. The egg can turn into a baby chick, which makes it a live thing. A hen is also a very good mother; she takes very good care of her chicks.

If you've ever watched a hen with her chickens, those babies follow her everywhere. When she talks, they listen. Sometimes our children get out of hand. They decide that they want to do things their way. There are times when their way is only going to lead them to trouble, but they don't see it. Fortunately, there's an old work that you can do to pull your children back closer to the nest.

You need a fresh hen egg for each child and a basket with fresh moss in it. Name each one of the eggs for a child, then carefully place the eggs on the bed of moss. Place them in a circle so you can put a seven-day candle in the center of the basket. Light the candle and pray Proverbs 1:8-9 over the candle three times a day for at least twenty-one days:

> 8 Listen, my son, to your father's instruction
> and do not forsake your mother's teaching.
>
> 9 They are a garland to grace your head
> and a chain to adorn your neck.

Once the work is over, bury the eggs at the front door of the home.

ROOSTERS

Roosters are also very powerful. The rooster belongs to St. Peter. St. Peter holds the keys to the gates of heaven. It is said that whatever St. Peter grants on earth is also granted in heaven. When I was young, St. Peter was the only saint I ever heard my mama talk about. It's from her that I learned about St. Peter and the rooster. (She is also the one who taught me how important the number three is.)

It is said in the Bible that St. Peter would betray Jesus before the rooster crowed three times. If you look at Matthew 26:33-35 and 69-74, it tells of St. Peter denying Jesus and Jesus telling him the rooster will not crow until he was denied three times:

33 Peter replied, "Even if all fall away on account of you, I never will."

34 "Truly I tell you," Jesus answered, "this very night, before the rooster crows, you will disown me three times."

35 But Peter declared, "Even if I have to die with you, I will never disown you." And all the other disciples said the same.

69 Now Peter was sitting out in the courtyard, and a servant girl came to him. "You also were with Jesus of Galilee," she said.

70 But he denied it before them all. "I don't know what you're talking about," he said.

71 Then he went out to the gateway, where another servant girl saw him and said to the people there, "This fellow was with Jesus of Nazareth."

72 He denied it again, with an oath: "I don't know the man!"

73 After a little while, those standing there went up to Peter and said, "Surely you are one of them; your accent gives you away."

74 Then he began to call down curses, and he swore to them, "I don't know the man!"

Roosters are naturally gifted for scratching up messes and giving warnings. I believe that it all goes back to St. Peter. He is a powerful healer and a road opener. When a rooster is scratching, he is scratching things up and out of the way, just like St. Peter removes things out of the way. Rooster feathers are really good for cleansings.

Roosters are very intelligent. I know this for fact, because I have chickens and I had a rooster that I called Houdini. I called him Houdini because when I first got him, I tried to keep him in a coop and every time I turned around he would escape. I had always wanted a rooster, and one time I had someone who needed some work to be done but they didn't have the money to pay me for the work, so we bartered and they gave me a baby rooster who became Houdini for payment. I believe he was a gift from spirit.

The thing about roosters is that not only are they highly intelligent, but they are very in tune with the energies that are moving around on the land that they call home. Houdini used to pick up rocks and line them up in front of the doorway leading outside. At first, I didn't know how those rocks were getting there. I thought someone was trying to set a trick for me. But one day I caught him doing it, and I was like, "Oh, OK, so you've got jokes over here you're working." So I started calling him Houdini the Conjure rooster. I came to realize that if I saw rocks laid out, then something was going on and I needed to do divination to find out what it was.

Houdini would also get on top of the house and start pecking and scratching up there. It sounded like he was trying to tear the roof off of the house. Once he felt it was enough, he would start crowing and fly down. If someone came here whose spirit was off, he would cut up the whole time they were here. It was like he could tell if something was off. He could tell if someone was throwing at me or my house. Anytime Houdini started acting funny, I knew to start cleansings and protections because something was fixing to come.

He used to fly up my back flapping his wings, and the first time that he did that it kind of scared me because I was like, "Is he attacking me?" But no. I feel like he was cleansing me, because once he was done making that pass up my back to my head he would just go on about his business. When I was doing a class, he would come to the breezeway to visit. He didn't cut up then; he would just watch and see what was going on.

My heart was broken when he passed. I used to place his stories on my Facebook page, and I think folks really enjoyed watching videos of him and seeing how he acted. In the time that he was here with me I learned a lot from him. I learned more about roosters dealing with him. We should never underestimate the power of the intelligence of animals.

Doves

The Bible has a lot of passages where they speak about doves. As a Conjure worker, I was taught that doves bring forth peace. In some of the passages in the Old Testament, it says that the doves moaned. Here are a few examples:

Isaiah 59:11

We all growl like bears;
  we moan mournfully like doves.
We look for justice, but find none;
  for deliverance, but it is far away.

As you can see, doves were given as strong offerings back then. The same is said of today's world. Many years ago, I had an elder cleanse me off with a dove. Once the cleansing was done, the dove was let go. I was told that I should never harm a dove, as the bird belongs to God. They should be petitioned and then set free to carry out the prayers. Doves are very holy birds.

Leviticus 15:14

On the eighth day he must take two doves or two young
pigeons and come before the LORD to the entrance to the tent
of meeting and give them to the priest.

Here is a love song. This can be worked over a red candle for a lover.

Song of Songs 5:2

I slept but my heart was awake.
  Listen! My beloved is knocking:
"Open to me, my sister, my darling,
  my dove, my flawless one.
My head is drenched with dew,
  my hair with the dampness of the night."

Owls

My mama believed that owls bring wisdom and death. To see an owl, she felt spirit was showing her something she needed to know; to hear an owl hoot at night, she felt like death was coming. My daughter to this day has a fear of owls. If she hears one hooting at night it scares her, no matter how hard I try to convince her that it doesn't always mean physical death. She trusts her grandma's wisdom more than mine where owls are concerned. Although I do believe that a hoot owl at night is telling of a death, like the Ace of Spades in a card deck or the Death card in the Tarot, I don't believe it is always physical death. It could mean that a big upset is coming but in the end things will be better.

Ravens

If you look in Luke 12:24, you will see that the raven neither reaps nor sows, and yet God takes care of the raven:

> Consider the ravens: They do not sow or reap, they have no storeroom or barn; yet God feeds them. And how much more valuable you are than birds!

THE PROPHET ELIJAH

I was taught that ravens are messengers and they belong to the Prophet Elijah. If you look at 1 Kings 17:2-6, you will see that God sent the ravens to feed the Prophet Elijah:

> 2 Then the word of the Lord came to Elijah: 3 "Leave here, turn eastward and hide in the Kerith Ravine, east of the Jordan. 4 You will drink from the brook, and I have directed the ravens to supply you with food there."
>
> 5 So he did what the Lord had told him. He went to the Kerith Ravine, east of the Jordan, and stayed there. 6 The ravens brought him bread and meat in the morning and bread and meat in the evening, and he drank from the brook.

As we look on in the chapter, we see that the Prophet Elijah was also given the gift to bring the dead back to life:

> 1 Kings 17:12-24
>
> 12 "As surely as the Lord your God lives," she replied, "I don't have any bread—only a handful of flour in a jar and a little olive oil in a jug. I am gathering a few sticks to take home

and make a meal for myself and my son, that we may eat it—and die."

13 Elijah said to her, "Don't be afraid. Go home and do as you have said. But first make a small loaf of bread for me from what you have and bring it to me, and then make something for yourself and your son. 14 For this is what the Lord, the God of Israel, says: 'The jar of flour will not be used up and the jug of oil will not run dry until the day the Lord sends rain on the land.'"

15 She went away and did as Elijah had told her. So there was food every day for Elijah and for the woman and her family. 16 For the jar of flour was not used up and the jug of oil did not run dry, in keeping with the word of the Lord spoken by Elijah.

17 Some time later the son of the woman who owned the house became ill. He grew worse and worse, and finally stopped breathing. 18 She said to Elijah, "What do you have against me, man of God? Did you come to remind me of my sin and kill my son?"

19 "Give me your son," Elijah replied. He took him from her arms, carried him to the upper room where he was staying, and laid him on his bed. 20 Then he cried out to the Lord, "Lord my God, have you brought tragedy even on this widow I am staying with, by causing her son to die?" 21 Then he stretched himself out on the boy three times and cried out to the Lord, "Lord my God, let this boy's life return to him!"

22 The Lord heard Elijah's cry, and the boy's life returned to him, and he lived. 23 Elijah picked up the child and carried him down from the room into the house. He gave him to his mother and said, "Look, your son is alive!"

24 Then the woman said to Elijah, "Now I know that you are a man of God and that the word of the Lord from your mouth is the truth."

Elijah is also the only man God gave permission to take a life of another person. He is very powerful and very much the prophet to go to when you are in danger, or when you need food because you are hungry. Just remember that whatever he gives, he also can take away.

Another thing that I have found teaching is that most folks don't know that the prophet Elijah didn't die! He was brought up to heaven in a ball of fire. If you look at 2 Kings 2:9-14, it tells how his clothes fell off of him and he was gone in a ball of fire:

9 When they had crossed, Elijah said to Elisha, "Tell me, what can I do for you before I am taken from you?"

"Let me inherit a double portion of your spirit," Elisha replied.

10 "You have asked a difficult thing," Elijah said, "yet if you see me when I am taken from you, it will be yours—otherwise, it will not."

11 As they were walking along and talking together, suddenly a chariot of fire and horses of fire appeared and separated the two of them, and Elijah went up to heaven in a whirlwind. 12 Elisha saw this and cried out, "My father! My father! The chariots and horsemen of Israel!" And Elisha saw him no more. Then he took hold of his garment and tore it in two.

13 Elisha then picked up Elijah's cloak that had fallen from him and went back and stood on the bank of the Jordan. 14 He took the cloak that had fallen from Elijah and struck the water with it. "Where now is the Lord, the God of Elijah?" he asked. When he struck the water, it divided to the right and to the left, and he crossed over.

So if we go by what is written in the Old Testament, we understand that the Prophet Elijah can heal the sick, feed the hungry, and kill a man. Fire is one of his elements. He is very powerful. I have worked with him since my early twenties and I will give you a little advice: Do not go to him over something that you shouldn't, like just because you don't like someone or because someone made you mad—he isn't the one to play with like that. If you need justice, give him a red candle and petition him. If you need cleansing, give him a blue candle and petition. But don't ask him to harm someone unjustly—it might just backfire on you.

These stories are important to young Conjure workers so they may know how to work with the prophets. From what I have seen, most new-age Conjure workers throw the Bible out even though the Old Testament has so many secrets in it that have been passed down from generation to generation of Conjure workers.

Red Birds

Old folks believe that red birds are messengers from the ancestors. They let us know our dead kin is safe and sound. It is also believed that they are sent by God to bring peace and blessings. Some elders say that the red bird is a symbol of God and represents the blood of Jesus. When you see one, they say you will receive a message from God.

Vultures

Vultures are another one of those birds that can tell when death is coming or when a cleansing is needed. They are one of my favorite birds. There are at least twenty different types of vultures, though, and you need to know the difference between them, because the black vulture is protected by law under the Migratory Bird Treaty Act of 1918. Under this law, black vultures and their nests and eggs can't be killed or destroyed without a permit.

Vultures are very powerful when it comes to cleansing works. They will clean the skin right off the bone of anything that is dead. They are also very cunning; they will circle their prey, watching and waiting for just the right time to swoop in. The old folks say they can smell death coming. I've seen them in yards just sitting there, looking around. This tells me that something or someone in that household is fixing to have a major upset or that death is waiting on someone who lives there. If I see a lone vulture feeding or flying overhead, I know it is time for a spiritual cleansing.

If you are lucky enough to be gifted a vulture feather, you can brush yourself down with the feather to do the cleansing. The spirit of the bird will eat away anything that is not good for your spirit. To do a brush down with a vulture feather or fan, you start at the crown of the head, swooping downward to the feet, and moving the feather or fan outward toward the ground. You move the feather or fan in one direction down and outward. If you move the fan back and forth over the body, then all you are doing is stirring up the mess you are trying to cleanse off of you. It doesn't matter what tool you are working with—when you are doing a cleansing, you always go in a downward motion. Once the cleansing is over, you should give an offering to the spirit of the bird. I usually give a stick candle, a cool glass of water, and a small piece of raw meat. I give the meat because that is how I was taught, but also because many birds eat raw meat. I was taught not to give the offering before the cleansing, because the spirit of the bird will get too full and there will be no room for what is being taken off.

Flies

Flies in the house are a sign of a crossed condition! If you have an infestation of flies in your home, then you need to burn some vesta powder (see page 164) to clear out whatever is there. Then you come back with some protection work and blessing work. Sometimes it takes a couple of cleansings to get the home clear and cleansed.

Nutria

Nutria are swamp rats that eat everything in sight and tunnel under everything. These beaverlike rodents can even cause erosion on the banks of a river. Their pelts are very expensive. If you can get a pelt, it is good for hiding works or even hiding yourself from an enemy. (Remember what I said about knowing the animals?)

I have a small bag made out of nutria pelt that a lady gave me as a gift. I use it as a working bag. It holds works of cleansing and protection work. Since nutria are usually out from dusk to daylight, those are the best times to work with them.

When I first met my husband almost forty-five years ago, he was a trapper. The man he worked for sold nutria pelts for a living. Folks still hunt them; they can destroy so much in a little bit of time.

Possums

Possum bones are good for reading bones. I read with a few possum bones I've had in my set of bones for many years. The possum is also good to work with when you are trying to hide. They are very good at playing dead. If you feel like you are being attacked by an enemy, you can do this work to hide your home and family from them:

A Spell to Hide

You need a four-by-four piece of red flannel, a photo of the front door of your home, a pinch of dirt from the four corners of the property and the front door, red cotton thread, two possum bones, whiskey, and four white stick candles.

Lay your photo down on the flannel and then place your dirt on top of it. Fold the flannel into a small packet and then use the red cotton string to bind the packet together. When you have the packet made, wrap the two bones around it, making sure to tie it off with three knots. Say your prayer over the packet as you tie each knot. Feed the packet a little whiskey, then place the packet on the table. Place the four stick candles in the order of top, bottom, left, right. Light the candles in the order you laid them out; say your prayer over each candle as you light it. When the candles burn, nail the packet above the front door of the home.

Live Things in You

My mama was a big believer that you could get worms by walking around barefoot. My mama believed that it was possible to get worms through the feet if you walked in the wrong place. When I was a child, twice a year my mama would treat us for worms. She would make us take a spoon of sugar with a drop or two of turpentine on it. We know today that turpentine is poisonous, but growing up it was a remedy that was used to keep so-called "live things" out of you.

Nowadays, folks make a big deal out of live things in you as part of a crossed condition in Conjure work. I had an elder tell me a story one time of a target being fed spider eggs. The eggs hatched in their stomach. These are stories that are passed down, from generation to generation. They teach us to watch what we eat and drink, to watch where we walk, to be mindful of who we let around our personal concerns. I am not saying that this is not true or that it's not possible. This started further back than I am old. Although there has been documentation of weird things happening inside the body (We now know that if pork is not cleaned and handled well, it can have worms in it; then people eat the pork and end up with worms, which are considered a crossed condition in Conjure.), when the elders talk about live things in you, they're mostly talking about worms.

Some folks believe that this is an old wives' tale. They believe that it's possible to feed someone live things that will grow inside of their bodies. Folks truly believe this. Is it possible? Yes, it is possible. Does it happen as often as some folks claim? No. And is it easy to achieve this crossed condition? No, it's not.

Do I believe that you can cross someone up with food and drink? Of course I do! I know it can happen! Some years ago some Conjure workers were fascinated with live things in you and so it kind of caused hysterics among some clients.

We as workers have a responsibility for the folks that we help. We are not doctors and we do not have that type of training to tell someone that they have live things running through their bodies; it is not our place to give that type of diagnosis. If someone comes to you with this type of ailment please refer them to get medical help.

PART IV

Tools of the Trade

In this part, I'm gonna touch on roots, herbs, and curios, because, I'll so shamelessly say, I wrote an herbal book before: *Hoodoo Herbal*. In this book you're holding in your hands now, I am gonna share some of my favorite herbs and curios that I like to work with. When you are starting this work, you don't need to invest a lot of money buying every single herb and root. Start out slow and use what you have.

13

Herbs and Roots

Herbs in the Bible

First, I want to talk about the herbs that can be found in the Bible. The Old Testament is full of works that can be worked to help yourself. I personally don't work much with the New Testament, because that's not how I was taught. You will also find that there are holy oils that are written about in the Bible, which we'll get to in a little bit. These oils and herbs can add great power to your work.

Hyssop

Did you know that hyssop is a holy herb? If you look in the Old Testament, you will see that it is alleged to add great power when doing works for cleansing and protection. Back in the times of the Bible, folks who were collecting the dead carried hyssop on them. If you look at Exodus 12:22, you will see it says that you should carry a bundle of hyssop:

> Take a bunch of hyssop, dip it into the blood in the basin and put some of the blood on the top and on both sides of the doorframe. None of you shall go out of the door of your house until morning.

If you read on to verse 23, this is where it talks about marking the doors:

When the Lord goes through the land to strike down the Egyptians, he will see the blood on the top and sides of the doorframe and will pass over that doorway, and he will not permit the destroyer to enter your houses and strike you down.

In that day and time, the doors were marked with blood to keep the house safe from God's justice. I just want to share that little bit of information because I think that it's important to know that the doors of your home should also be marked when you cleanse them.

A bath made with hyssop is a powerful cleansing bath, and hyssop oil is a great protection oil. If you look in Psalms 51:7, it again gives the instructions to wash yourself with hyssop and you will be washed clean:

Cleanse me with hyssop, and I will be clean;
wash me, and I will be whiter than snow.

Mandrake

Mandrake is another root that can be found in the Bible. Back in the day and time of the Old Testament, mandrake root could be bartered with or used as a tool. If you look in Genesis 30:14-16, you can see how the mandrake root was used:

14 During wheat harvest, Reuben went out into the fields and found some mandrake plants, which he brought to his mother Leah. Rachel said to Leah, "Please give me some of your son's mandrakes."

15 But she said to her, "Wasn't it enough that you took away my husband? Will you take my son's mandrakes too?"

"Very well," Rachel said, "he can sleep with you tonight in return for your son's mandrakes."

16 So when Jacob came in from the fields that evening, Leah went out to meet him. "You must sleep with me," she said. "I have hired you with my son's mandrakes." So he slept with her that night.

More Herbs in the Bible

There are many other herbs that can be found within the pages of the Bible. Here are just a few of them.

BALM OF GILEAD

Jeremiah 46:11

"Go up to Gilead and get balm,
*   Virgin Daughter Egypt.*
But you try many medicines in vain;
*   there is no healing for you.*

CINNAMON

Exodus 30:23

"Take the following fine spices: 500 shekels of liquid myrrh, half as much (that is, 250 shekels) of fragrant cinnamon, 250 shekels of fragrant calamus,

CORIANDER

Exodus 16:31

The people of Israel called the bread manna. It was white like coriander seed and tasted like wafers made with honey.

CUMIN

Mathew 23:23

"Woe to you, teachers of the law and Pharisees, you hypocrites! You give a tenth of your spices—mint, dill and cumin. But you have neglected the more important matters of the law—justice, mercy and faithfulness. You should have practiced the latter, without neglecting the former.

Isaiah 28:25

When he has leveled the surface,
*   does he not sow caraway and scatter cumin?*
Does he not plant wheat in its place,

> *barley in its plot,*
> *and spelt in its field?*

DILL

Matthew 23:23

"Woe to you, teachers of the law and Pharisees, you hypocrites! You give a tenth of your spices—mint, dill and cumin. But you have neglected the more important matters of the law—justice, mercy and faithfulness. You should have practiced the latter, without neglecting the former.

GARLIC

Numbers 11:5

We remember the fish we ate in Egypt at no cost—also the cucumbers, melons, leeks, onions and garlic.

MINT

Mathew 23:23

"Woe to you, teachers of the law and Pharisees, you hypocrites! You give a tenth of your spices—mint, dill and cumin. But you have neglected the more important matters of the law—justice, mercy and faithfulness. You should have practiced the latter, without neglecting the former.

Luke 11:42

"Woe to you Pharisees, because you give God a tenth of your mint, rue [ruda] and all other kinds of garden herbs, but you neglect justice and the love of God. You should have practiced the latter without leaving the former undone.

MUSTARD SEED

Matthew 13:31-32

31 He told them another parable: "The kingdom of heaven is like a mustard seed, which a man took and planted in his field. 32 Though it is the smallest of all seeds, yet when it grows, it is the largest of garden plants and becomes a tree, so that the birds come and perch in its branches."

RUDA

Luke 11:42

"Woe to you Pharisees, because you give God a tenth of your mint, rue [ruda] and all other kinds of garden herbs, but you neglect justice and the love of God. You should have practiced the latter without leaving the former undone.

Not Today, Satan

I want to share this little bit of information before I move on and get into the herbs and what they can be worked for. In the South you might hear somebody say, "Not today, Satan." Well they're not exactly talking about the devil in the Bible; they are talking about anything that is going to upset their day, from an argument to a flat tire.

Within this work you are going to see products that are called Run Devil Run products. These products are worked with to send the devil running per se. So when you put these products together, any root or herb that you see that has the word *devil* in it can be added to the ingredients in these types of work. You have devil's bit, devil's dung, devil's pod, and devil's shoestring (which is one of my favorite herbs to work with). The old folks say that devil's shoestring can be worked with to hobble the devil, to hold him down.

Devil's Shoestring Working for Protection

Devil's shoestring is one of my favorite herbs, so I wanted to give you a little work that you can do with it. This may seem like a simple work, but it is very powerful.

You will need three pieces of devil's shoestring, each about three inches long; a photo of your home; and some red cotton string.

Across the front of the photo of your home, write your petition. Then roll the photo toward you while praying for protection for your home. Take that packet and put it between the three devil's shoestrings, then wrap it with the red cotton thread so it's all held together. As you are wrapping the thread around the packet and the root, you say your prayer and your petition that your home be protected.

Once it's wrapped, then you tie three knots. On each knot you say your prayer and your petition. You can take that packet and put it above your door for protection of your home.

Common Herbs and Roots I Work With

This is by no means a full list of herbs and roots, but it is a list that I work with often. If you want a full list of roots in herbs that you can work with, then you need to buy yourself a good herbal (I suggest my book *Hoodoo Herbal*). I just want to touch on these to give you a good foundation to start with.

Allheal can be added to baths for healing. It is also good when added to packets to keep sickness away.

Aloe is a very bitter herb that is added to Shut Your Mouth products and also added to works to stop gossip.

Alum is another one that can be worked with to stop gossip, but it is also good for removing cross conditions.

Angelica root, or what some call the Holy Ghost root, is the root of the angels. It is worked with for protection, when dealing with children who will not listen, and other family issues.

Asafoetida stinks to high heaven. The old folks say that even the devil can't stand the smell of it, so this herb is worked with for Run Devil Run work and removing any cross condition.

Balm of Gilead, like lavender, is one of my favorite herbs to work with when I'm doing peaceful home work or works to bring peace. It soothes hurt feelings and is also good when you are doing cut and clear work.

Barberry does exactly what the name implies: it bars things, stops them. This is a must-have in your cabinet. You can mix barberry, the dirt from the four corners of the crossroads, and dirt from a stop sign to stop your enemies in their tracks.

Basil can be worked with for cleansings, to send evil away, for protection, and for healing. It is one of my favorite herbs to work with.

Bayberry is good for better business works, for drawing money into your pocket. There's a little rhyme that says, "Bayberry candle burned to the socket will put money into your pocket." It is a powerful money herb.

Bay leaf is good for protection and cleansing. A bay leaf placed behind the door will protect the home. One placed in every corner of the home will also offer protection. They are also good to add to cleansing baths and washes.

Blackberry leaves are worked with for all reversal work. They return the evil back to the sender. It is an important herb to have in your cabinet.

Bloodroot is worked with for all types of works dealing with your children or your family. It is good to add to peaceful home works.

Broom straw is good for all types of cleansing work and protection work, and it's worked with to remove cross conditions.

Calamus root is worked with for all domination work or controlling works, such as Do as I Say works.

Cayenne pepper is added to heat things up. It puts fire in any work. Cayenne pepper should never be added to peaceful home types of work because it's just going to heat up the temperament that's already going on in the home.

Couch grass can be worked with along with barberry to bind your enemies.

Deer's-tongue is worked with in court cases when you want to charm someone in love work. It helps you speak with eloquence.

Eyebright is worked with as a wash to heal your eyes, but it also works well with St. Lucy when you are trying to see what is going on. It works on anything that has to do with the eyes or seeing.

Five finger grass does anything that the five fingers on a hand can do, which makes it perfect for all types of money works and works where you are trying to draw something into your hands.

Gumbo filé is good for all money work, prosperity work, and success work.

Jezebel root is worked with to make a man give you his money and for domination. It is another one of my favorite roots.

Job's tears are very powerful. They say that if you work seven seeds for seven days, they will make your wishes come true. On the other side of that, they can make your enemies shed tears.

Knotweed is worked with for all blocking and binding works.

Licorice root is worked with in all workings where you need power, strength to be in control, and to have domination over the situation. It is one of my all-time favorite roots.

Life Everlasting is good to add to all healing works. The old folks say that this herb will help you live a longer life.

Lovage root not only draws in love but also promotes self-love and should be added to all love works and healing works. A must for your cabinet.

Lucky hand root is added to all money works and is good for gambling. It is said to be a very lucky root.

Master of the woods is good for all domination, controlling, and Do as I Say work.

Master root helps you take charge. It is great for all works that you need the upper hand in.

Motherwort is good for all types of work that is concerning your children or grandchildren.

Black mustard seeds cause confusion and loss of concentration when the work is being done on a target.

Nutmeg is worked with all money matters and all things dealing with prosperity and good fortune.

Orange peel is worked with for all attraction works. It is one of the main ingredients in attraction products and road-opening products.

Queen Elizabeth root is worked with by women to draw power, love, luck, and the opposite sex. It also adds to a woman's personal power.

Ruda is worked with to remove all cross conditions. It can add power to the work. It can be worked with to destroy an enemy. It is good to grow ruda around your home to protect your home.

Self-heal is worked in all health matters and is said to help cleanse.

Snakeroot is worked with to stop gossip. It will also protect you against false friends. Everyone should have some of this planted at their homes. It's easy to grow.

Solomon's seal root is named after King Solomon in the Bible and brings forth wisdom and power and adds protection in all Conjure work.

Spanish moss can be worked with to protect your money, your home—but it can also be worked with to nail an enemy down.

Tobacco can be used as an offering or to hold an enemy down.

Walnut is worked with to remove jinxes and cross conditions. It can also be helpful with breakup work.

Willow is worked with to help remove cross conditions and also to place a jinx on a target.

14

Curios

There are many different curios that are worked with in Conjure. Some of my favorites are the alligator claw, chicken feet, turkey feet, any type of bone . . . the list could go on forever. These things are worked with to add power to the work you are doing. Nails, mirrors, and needles are also worked with in this work.

Really, anything can be added to this work if you understand what that thing does. For example, the monkey paw is said to draw in prosperity and anything that you ask for. It can also be worked to jinx a target. But you wouldn't want to put a snakeskin in with your money work—that might not turn out well for you. If, however, you are looking for wisdom or if you are trying to find out information, then a snakeskin would be perfect to work with. You really need to have some knowledge of the things that you will be working with.

There are many things around your house that can be used in Conjure. My grandma kept a Bible opened in the bedroom and an old, rusted sifter under each bed. When I asked her about the sifter, which I removed one time, she had a fit. She said, "A haunt can't haunt until they count all the holes in the sifter; and they can't count that high—they lose track of the numbers!" Needless to say, I have never forgotten it, and if you look under my bed, you will find an open Bible with a sifter sitting on top of it. No one told me this was Conjure work for protection. It was said to be an old wives' tale that some folks believed in, yet it is a living Conjure.

The elders used what they had. It doesn't take a lot. If all you had was a pair of scissors to do a cleansing or protection working for your home, then all you would have to do is go around your body (about two inches away from your body because you don't want to cut yourself) and just start acting like you're cutting. That will cut away whatever is there. Then you take those same scissors, open them up, and hang them behind the door of your home for protection.

Keys are another big item in Conjure work. Look at all the things that a key can do—it can open a door; it can lock a door. So keys are perfect to hang beside your door to keep your roads open. Remember that the keys belong to St. Peter, and St. Peter holds the keys to heaven, and whatever he grants in heaven is also granted on earth.

Just look around your home and you will be surprised at the things that you already have that you can work with. Don't go spending a whole lot of money at once. Use what you have around the house.

Blades and Scissors

Blades and scissors have been worked with in Conjure work for as long as there has been Conjure. Back in the day, when the elders didn't have much, they always had some type of blade and a pair of scissors. As we know, scissors are used for cutting things, and a blade is also used for chopping and cutting. They make great tools for doing Conjure work, for cutting and clearing, for removing, and for holding the target down. They are an important tool to have when doing Conjure works. Blades and scissors are both worked with for the protection of the home and the Conjure worker. Some workers will also work with them to cut away crossed conditions, hexes, or jinxes.

Blades

Blades, such as knives and machetes, can be worked with in cleansings to cut away blocks and crossed conditions. They can be worked with in a spiritual battle when one is being attacked by a spiritual enemy.

If you feel your home needs to be protected, you should clean the doors inside and out. Dress them with a protection wash, then place a blade standing upward behind the main door of the house. Placing the blade upward is to cut away anything negative that tries to get into the home; it will even cut away negativity on folks that are going in and out of the house.

Over the years, I have been taught many works working with blades. Some seem simple, but trust me, they are powerful works. Don't let the simplicity of the work fool you. I'm going to share one of the simplest ones I know. It is one of my favorites to work with.

You need a thin blade knife and a photo of the target. All you have to do is place the photo upside down and run the blade through it. Leave the photo on the blade. Say your petition and prayer of what you need to happen to the target, and then either place the blade upward to cut them away from you, or place the blade downward to not only cut them away from you but also cut their luck and hold them down.

Scissors

Scissors are also good to keep unwanted things out of your home. You can place an open pair of scissors facing upward at the front door for protection, or you can place them facing downward to cut things that might be trying to get into the house. You should never point a pair of scissors at anyone you love, though—it is said that to do so will cut the bond between you. In fact, you should always be careful how you handle all blades and scissors around folks you love, because they can cut the love you feel for each other.

Scissors, like brooms, being kept open by the front door is a cultural thing in the South. Folks don't even realize that it is part of Conjure work. They do it because their grandmas did it and they were raised on tales of the boo hags and the plat-eye. It is said to keep the devil and the boo hags out of the house.

I grew up on stories of the boo hag. Back when I was growing up, folks slept with the doors and windows open. There wasn't any air conditioning—my grandma didn't even have a fan. Her bedroom was large and there were two beds in the room. There were two windows in the room, but the beds were placed away from them because it was believed that the boo hag could come in through the open windows and you didn't want to be sleeping nearby. I was raised to believe that the boo hag would come into the room while we were sleeping and steal our breath away so they could live. They only come out at night and cannot be in the light of day. They need the breath and the skin of their target to live. If we woke up tired or didn't sleep well, my grandma would say, "Guess the ole hag was riding last night!"

Scissors are also worked with in cut and clear works; they cut away whatever is being removed.

Cut and Clear Working

There are many different ways a worker could do a cut and clear, but I'm going to share with you one of my favorites. This is a tried-and-true method.

You need about a foot of cotton twine, a photo of the target, and two nine-day candles. Find the center of the twine, make it into a loose knot, hold the knot up to your mouth, and say, "[Name] is bound within this knot. When the twine is cut, they will be cut away from me till the end of days."

Pull the knot tight, then cleanse yourself with the twine going from head to toe, praying that the target be bound from you forever and a day.

Tie the end of the twine around each candle. Place the candles where they are touching with the twine between them. Light the first candle, which represents you, and pray your petition over it. Then light the other candle for the target and pray the petition over it.

Every day, move the target's candle a little bit away from your candle. When the twine is stretched out tight, take a pair of scissors and cut the twine above the knot on your side. The knot will be on the target's side.

Continue moving the target away from you each day until the candles burn out. Once the candles are out, bury the target's twine and container in the west when the sun is almost down. Your candle can be taken to the woods and left there with an offering of your choice.

If you are initiated in something spiritual, you should be careful when cutting and clearing around your head. I know this because my godfather, Papa Hector Salva, told me. I started my journey in the 21 Divisions, or what some call Dominican Vodou, on August 30, 2020, under my godfather. I got initiated for personal reasons, but I am a

Conjure woman through and through. It is my life. It is who I am and what I know.

Just like with all Conjure work, you need to be careful. Like I said, it may seem simple (and it is), but it is also very powerful. You should always make sure the work is justified. No work should be done on anyone without divination being done first. If you are wrong and hit the wrong person, you could be hit with your own work. You and you alone are responsible for the works you do. And always remember, every action causes a reaction. Be mindful and always work with a cool head, not when you are upset.

Bottles and Jars

One time, I was in the kitchen talking to my oldest granddaughter about boys. Her little sister was sitting on the floor in front of the kitchen sink just listening. So I guess my granddaughter was probably about twelve, maybe, and her uncle, my baby boy, had friends who would come and hang out here at the house. So I was telling my granddaughter, "Be careful, because those boys are older, you know . . ." I think she might have had a crush on one of them. These are all boys that my son has hung out with since they started going to school. I'm just talking to her and minding my own business, when all of a sudden her sister says, "Well, mawmaw, if you're worried about it, why don't you just put him in a jar and go throw him in the river?"

Well, this got my attention! I said, "What do you know about a hotfoot jar, and where did you hear that at?"

She proceeds to tell me that all I needed to do was get a jar, put his foot track in it with some red pepper, say my prayers over it, and go throw it in the river.

Now I'm thinking, *Who in the world is telling my young granddaughter how to hotfoot somebody?* So once again I asked her, "Who told you about the hotfoot jar?"

"Well, you did, mawmaw."

I was shocked! "When did I tell you about the hotfoot jar?"

"Well, you didn't in so many words," she said. "But I heard you talking to one of the people you help, and I remembered what you said."

I didn't know what to say. I mean, really, what can you say? She heard me giving instructions to one of my clients on how to hotfoot someone and so she now knows how to do a hotfoot work. This is how they learn. I never knew that those kids were listening to me and my clients, but apparently they were.

I personally like working with containers, specifically bottles and jars (and yes, sometimes even hotfoot jars), because the more you work that work, the more the power of the work builds inside of that bottle or jar, and the more powerful the work becomes. I don't believe that you can just put a bunch of ingredients into a bottle or a jar and it's going to have long-term success if you just set it on a shelf somewhere and leave it. In order for your work to be a success, the work inside of it needs to move around, and you do this by shaking that jar or bottle daily while you are saying your prayers and petitions. If you just let the work sit there, it becomes stagnant, and, as we know, things that become stagnant no longer work.

This is one of my issues that I have with making honey jars, because when the honey gets old it crystallizes, and whatever is in that jar is stuck in place. Now, if you're doing love work, that might be a great thing. But if you're doing a different type of work where you're trying to draw prosperity into your life or get rid of someone or something, then leaving that work just sitting there is not a very good idea. It's not going to work for long. And I know some workers get aggravated with me about the honey, but it's not something that I've made up. This is what I've seen, and this is what I know will happen. I do add a spoon of honey to some of my sweetening works, but that's all, because anything more and it's going to crystallize my work as time goes by.

Working with a Bottle or Jar

If you decide that you want to do some work in a bottle or a jar, I'm going to give you the basics of how to get the container ready for the ingredients you will add.

The first step is that your container needs to be washed well. This is important, because they do pick up energies from folks who have handled them in the past, and you don't want that in your work. I always wash mine with good hot, soapy water with a little bit of bleach in the water. Then I'll let them air-dry.

After they are physically cleansed, then I come back and I spiritually cleanse them. You can do this simply by wiping them down with Florida Water or some type of spiritual water that you've made. Once again, you let them air-dry. I usually let mine sit until the next day, because if you don't let them dry all the way, moisture will be left inside your jar and it can cause mold in your work. So it's better just to take the time and let them dry well before you decide to load them and work with them.

Once you have the jar ready and you've decided exactly what you're going to work with the jar for, you need to say your prayer inside that jar. You do this by blowing into the jar as you are praying, and then you literally blow three breaths inside that jar. The breaths are important because our breath keeps us alive.

Then it is time to add your ingredients into the jar, and as you already know, your prayer should be said over the work three times each along with your breath. Then you load everything into your jar, you put the lid on the jar, shake the jar up while you're saying your prayer and your petition, and then you need to either start burning candles on top of your jar or set your jar into some type of candle setup. From there, you work your jar daily.

You cannot but just work that jar one or two times and expect the jar to continue working. You need to work that jar daily or you will just be wasting your time, spirit's time, and the money it cost you to make the jar. Conjure is called *work* because it takes work to get success. So if you are going to be a Conjure worker, get ready to work.

Blue Bottle Trees

You may be asking yourself, What in the world is a blue bottle tree, and what does a blue bottle tree have to do with Conjure work? The answer is, Everything! The blue bottle tree is a simple but powerful way to protect your home and they are beautiful. There are two ways to do a blue bottle tree. One is to hang the bottles from the limb of a tree, and the other is to run the limb of the tree through the bottle. Either way will work. If you decide to make a blue bottle tree, you can hang them from a real tree or you can buy one of the ready-made iron trees. Either type of tree will work, and they both hold power.

Folks raised outside of the culture might not understand why the color blue is so important. What does a bottle tree do and why exactly do some folks have them hanging from the trees in their yards or on iron trees? Most folks from the South know the answer to that question. We grow up with haunt blue, which is said to keep the haunts and ghosts away from the house. Haunts can't cross over water, and it is believed they don't know the difference between the blue in the paint or bottles and the blue of the water, so they stay away from the homes that have the ceiling of the porch painted blue or have blue bottles hanging in the trees.

I had a blue bottle tree for many years in my garden until a hurricane came and the winds busted all my bottles. We had other hurricanes that never broke a bottle, but this one broke all of them. I feel like they were full and had done their job. I am now working on starting a new bottle tree. It's slow going because it's kind of hard to find blue bottles nowadays.

Nowadays, folks will use a wrought iron tree to put their bottles on to protect their home from haunts and spirits that roam the land. Iron in itself is good for protection; this is why if you drive in the country, you might see old farm equipment left in fields by the road. The equipment is left there to rust because rust from iron is protective. That's one of the reasons rusty nails are worked with in Conjure.

There are a few steps to take before placing the bottles on the tree. Almost everything in Conjure deals with petitions and prayers or the cleansing of a tool before you work with it. The bottles need to be cleansed before you can place them on the tree.

When I was growing up, there was no running water in the house. The water came from a water well with a hand pump. Of course, today we all have running water, which is a blessing. You can cleanse your blue bottles by putting them under some cool running tap water. The cold water will remove anything that the glass might have picked up from folks handling it. Once you have all the bottles spiritually cleansed, then you just let them air-dry.

Once the bottles are dry, you will need to hold each bottle up to your mouth one at a time and say your petition and prayer over them for protection. Do not pray the prayer and petition into the bottle—pray it over the bottles. If you pray it into the bottle, then you are filling the bottle up and there will be no room to catch the haunts and spirits that are roaming around your home.

When you have the bottles ready, then it's time to place them on your tree. You can either tie the bottles to the limb with cotton string so they will be hanging down or you can stick the bottle on the limb.

P Casas and the Turkey Foot

I have a small altar set up in my kitchen where I have a few tools sitting on it. One day, the twins came for visit, and P Casas spotted a turkey foot on the altar and of course wanted to know what it was for. He asked me if he could pick it up, and I said yes, so he brought it to me and he started asking a million and one questions: Why did I have it? What was it for? What did it do? He's only three, but he will ask a ton of questions and he'll ask them over and over until he is satisfied with your answer. Now, they grew up here, so they're used to all the altars and candles burning and things that are different that other folks might not have, and I don't mind them touching my stuff because I know that they are drawn to it. Because of the weather change my knee was bothering me that day, so when he brought the turkey foot over to me I explained to him what it was for, why I had it. I showed him how to work with the foot for cleansing. Then I let him run the foot over my knee. I told him that he needed to say a prayer that my knee feel better and that the pain would be gone. He was so cute.

This is how young children learn. They're never too young to start learning. My children and my grandchildren have grown up with me working. They're used to it. My children and my grandchildren will come to the altars over here and light candles and say prayers when they need them. I know sometimes they even help their friends when they have issues and things going on. This work is supposed to be passed down, it's supposed to be shared within the families, and explaining to children when they ask questions is a good way to pass down the knowledge through the family. In my family, this work is intertwined in our daily lives. It's what we do. It's who we are.

Both chicken feet and turkey feet are worked with for cleansing and for protection. You can also work with them in prosperity works, but let's look at the cleansing and protection first.

Cleansing and Protection

The first thing that you need to do when you are working with any part of an animal is to look at that animal and see exactly what their characteristics are and how they maneuver in the world. The reason that I am putting the chicken feet and the turkey feet together instead of writing about them separately is because they both basically have the same characteristics. They both scratch; they are both highly intelligent.

The reason that chicken feet work so well for cleansing and protection and for drawing in money is because that's what chickens do all day long—they scratch and they move things around. So if you're doing a cleansing, that foot is going to pull things off of you and move them away from you as you're going down and out away from your body. Chicken feet are very protective because those claws are razor-sharp and they can draw blood. In the same instance, if you fix a chicken foot for money and prosperity, it is a great tool to work with for the simple reason that chickens scratch and dig all day long to find food.

I'm going to give an instruction on how to brush yourself down. Some of y'all who read this may already know how to do it, but I wanted to place it here for those who don't know how.

A Basic Brushdown

When you're going to do a brushdown, you should put a little bit of spiritual water —just a little spritz—on the foot. This could be a water that you've made yourself, or it could just be Florida Water. Either way, it's going to be OK. You start at the top of your head and you work your way down. Start in the front, go all the way down to your feet, and then outward so you're pulling whatever you're taking off and you're throwing it outward for the earth to take it.

Now before I go any further, let me say this: About fifteen years ago, I was doing a class somewhere and a lady who came to the class was adamant that you have to do something special in order to get rid of the energies that you are pulling off of someone so they don't get on someone else. This took up about twenty minutes of the class time, and I finally got her to understand that when you go down and you push whatever it is that you're taking off, it's going to go to the earth—it's not going to start running around having a party getting on everybody. I'm not a new-age worker, I'm an old-school worker. This is how I was taught, and this is how I've been doing Conjure since I was seventeen years old—fifty-plus years.

When you are cleansing, you are praying while you are doing it. You are petitioning spirit to take whatever is being removed and take it away. You're not just doing the actions and not just saying prayers, so if I thought that spirit wasn't truly removing and taking away whatever is being taken off, then I would have to believe that spirit does not do their job. I will absolutely never do this, because they have shown me in my lifetime what they are capable of doing—the blessings that they are capable of, the healings, the discernment that they have shown me. So faith has to be a part of this or you're wasting your time. You need to find something else to do if you don't have the faith that it takes to believe in yourself, number one, and to believe that the spirits that walk with you are going to help you in your work, number two. You will be wasting your time and their time.

So you continue going all over your body as far as you can reach, going downward in the same motion. You don't literally scratch your body with the chicken foot—you can hold it about two inches away from your body. Two inches away from the body is still going to start up that outer spirit that walks with us and protects us. I call it the catchall, because that's our first defense against cross conditions, jealousy, envy, or anything that is not in tune with us that might try to attach itself to us. You have to start up whatever is there in order to be able to get it off of you. I do have some students who literally will scratch themselves with the feet to remove whatever is there, but that really isn't necessary.

When you are finished with your cleansing, you need to take some type of oil (it can be any type of oil you have on hand) and you need to dress the crown of your head, your third eye, over your heart, the creases in your elbows, the creases behind your knees, and the bottoms of your feet from toe to heel and then your hands.

Protection Working

If you want to work a chicken foot or a turkey foot for protection, the best way is to dry them yourself. But you can buy one that is already cured. Put it on your altar and work with it. Say your prayers and petitions over it.

The one good thing I love about working with turkey feet is that the turkey gobbles up everything in sight, and the spirit of the turkey does not mind going into battle; it is powerful. So it is a very good tool to have when you're doing protection works. That said, the chicken foot is good for protection because chickens are good at discerning what is going on around you. So they both have their place.

Prosperity Working

I want to give you a working with a turkey foot for prosperity. Like I said, I like working with turkey feet because the turkeys gobble everything up.

The first thing you need to do is to get a turkey foot. You can either get one that's dried already or you can dry one yourself. I personally prefer to dry them myself because you can set something heavy on it and have the hand open. (I'm calling it a hand even though it's a foot because once it's opened up it looks like a hand.)

Once you have your foot ready, you need to cut a piece of flannel about three by three inches. You are also going to need some red cotton string, a white stick candle, gumbo filé or sasssafras powder, three coins out of your wallet, a small magnet, blue flag root, some shredded money, and maybe some lodestones or magnets, if you like. (Some workers like to work with lodestones. When I was a young worker, I learned to work with magnets. I like working with magnets because they have a stronger pull to them.) You also need to add something personal to the packet that we are fixing to make—the hair from the crown of your head is really good to add to your work, because that's where your spirit sits.

Once you have all your items together, get a cool glass of water, light your candle, say your prayer and your petition over each ingredient, and add it to your red flannel square. Once all the ingredients have been prayed over, then you're going to pray over them three more times before you close the packet up.

The easiest way to make a packet is to grab the four corners of the flannel, pull it up where you have a little ball, and then wrap your red thread around the top to hold the packet closed. On each wrap, you say your prayer and your petition.

Once you have the packet wrapped, you are going to tie three knots. On each knot, you are once again going to say your prayers and your petitions. Once you have the packet made, set it in front of your candle and let it go finish burning out. Say your prayer and petition over that packet three times and feed the packet some whiskey.

Let it rest for twenty-four hours. The next day, light another stick candle. Have a fresh glass of water. And now you are going to pray over your packet. You're going to say your prayer and petition over the foot and you are going to bond that packet to that foot, to the palm of the turkey's hand, To do this, you simply wrap it with red cotton thread. Once it's wrapped, you tie your three knots with your prayers on each knot and you feed it some whiskey. Place it in front of the candle. Let the candle burn out.

You now have a tool to draw prosperity, luck, and better business into your life. Just make sure that you feed it at least once a week. You can feed it with whiskey or some type of Conjure—it all depends on what you want to feed it with. The more you work that foot, the stronger it is going to become.

Over time, I believe that tools will become loaded down after you've worked with them for so long. A way to clean your chicken or turkey feet is to cover them with rock salt overnight. And then you just take them out, dust them off, and they're ready for the next time you need them.

PART V

Make It Yourself— Oils, Washes, Powders, and Candles

There may come a time when you want to make your own products—your own oils, washes, powders, and candles. I hope that this information will give you a foundation to be able to create your own recipes and your own products. There is nothing more powerful than to make the tools that you work with in this work. Don't get me wrong, there are a lot of good products out there, and I'll even pat myself on the back and say that I think that some of my products are the best on the market. But they still don't beat someone making their own products, saying their own prayers, and putting their own energy into what is being made. I've written about this in my other books too, so if making your own products is something that interests you, I recommend picking up *Hoodoo Herbal* and *Hoodoo Your Love*.

15

Oils

When I was coming up as a young Conjure worker, we didn't have all these different types of oils like we have today. I was taught to make spiritual oils out of olive oil or lard. Today, you have many choices of the types of oil that you work with to make your spiritual oils: almond oil; castor oil; coconut oil; grapeseed oil; jojoba oil; mineral oil; sunflower seed oil; or sweet oil, which is a refined olive oil. I'm just going to give you a quick list because you might not want to make your oils out of olive oil, even though that is the traditional way of making spiritual oils. You will find times when you might need to work with even other oils outside those in this list. For example, used motor oil is worked with when you want to jinx or hex someone. Castor oil and mineral oil are most of the time worked with for cross conditions.

Spiritual oils are an easy way to lay a trick on someone because you can dress the doors, you can dress their shoes, you can dress their clothes with the oil, and they will never know it. This work is called laying tricks because that is a large part of the work.

I'm going to give you instructions on how to make your own oils the old way that I was first taught to make them, and the new way that I learned to make them as I learned more Conjure.

Anointing oil can be worked with for dressing the doors, dressing yourself, dressing the windows. You can dress your vehicles for protection with it . . . the list just goes on and on. I'm going to give you a few examples and a few chapters and verses of how the oil was worked with back in biblical times.

Anointing Oil in the Bible

If you look in the Bible in Exodus 30:22-29, you will find the recipe for anointing oil:

> *22 Then the Lord said to Moses, 23 "Take the following fine spices: 500 shekels of liquid myrrh, half as much (that is, 250 shekels) of fragrant cinnamon, 250 shekels of fragrant calamus, 24 500 shekels of cassia—all according to the sanctuary shekel—and a hin of olive oil. 25 Make these into a sacred anointing oil, a fragrant blend, the work of a perfumer. It will be the sacred anointing oil. 26 Then use it to anoint the tent of meeting, the ark of the covenant law, 27 the table and all its articles, the lampstand and its accessories, the altar of incense, 28 the altar of burnt offering and all its utensils, and the basin with its stand. 29 You shall consecrate them so they will be most holy, and whatever touches them will be holy.*

The recipe for anointing oil is myrrh, cinnamon, and calamus, and you mix this in olive oil. If you look at the recipe, it calls for cinnamon and also cassia, which is a type of cinnamon. Cassia comes from China, and it's called Chinese cinnamon. So, using this recipe, you're actually adding two types of cinnamon. There are a lot of roots and herbs that were used in the Bible that have come into Conjure via the elders. If the elders have worked with the Bible all these years in Conjure, I feel like you can't go wrong following in their footsteps.

A side note: Some folks call it *anointing* oil. I was taught that the word used is *dressing*, because you are putting the oil on top of something; you're dressing it. But either way will work. The Bible says that it's anointing, so you can use whichever phrase you want to use. But when I talk about dressing something within my writings, I mean anointing.

The next step is to know how to dress or anoint someone when you are doing spiritual work. There are verses in the Bible that explain to you how to dress—or, rather, anoint, as the Bible calls it—someone whom you are blessing. You could even call it consecrating an item or a person. The Bible seems to like to use the word *consecrating*, and if you look in Leviticus 8:10, it shows us that Moses anointed the tabernacle and everything that was in there—altars, benches, everything was dressed and because of the anointing they became consecrated:

> *Then Moses took the anointing oil and anointed the tabernacle and everything in it, and so consecrated them.*

So the next question would be, how to dress something or someone with the oil? There are a few different ways to dress someone with the spiritual oil or blessing oil. Once again, I want to show you some examples out of the Bible just so you can see how the Bible and Conjure basically work on the same level when it comes to dressing oils.

I want to look at Exodus 29:21:

> *And take some blood from the altar and some of the anointing oil and sprinkle it on Aaron and his garments and on his sons and their garments. Then he and his sons and their garments will be consecrated.*

So this talks about Aaron and his sons and how they were anointed with oil. From this chapter in this verse, it looks like there had been a blood sacrifice given on the altar and so they took some of that blood and mixed it with the anointing oil and that is what they dressed Aaron and his sons with. If you look at the verse, it tells us that they not only dressed Aaron and his sons, but they also dressed the garments—the clothes, in modern terms—that they were wearing. Now in Conjure work there are many of old works where a target's shirt collars are dressed with some type of condition oil. Most of the time it was an oil to get control and to dominate the target, but the clothes were dressed just like in Exodus 29:21.

If you look at Leviticus 8:30, you see that Moses sprinkled anointing oil on Aaron's garments and also on his sons and his sons' garments:

> *Then Moses took some of the anointing oil and some of the blood from the altar and sprinkled them on Aaron and his garments and on his sons and their garments. So he*

consecrated Aaron and his garments and his sons and their garments.

I'm sure those aren't the only verses where someone is being anointed, but these two verses make me believe that this is a traditional way of dressing a person. This had to have been passed down to the elders that came before me, because I got this knowledge from my elders. I think that once the elders and ancestors of this work were forced into Christianity, they found all this information in the Old Testament and made it work for them. This is not a new-age concept about anointing and dressing to bring on blessings or to remove something from you.

Now I want to look at what is anointed—what can you anoint and bless. I found two chapters and verses in the Bible, and I want to talk about both of them because they both run along the same lines, which then shows us that this must have been the traditional way to anoint something in the times of the Bible, and this is how I was taught to dress the doors, the windows, and my home.

If you look at Exodus 40:9, you will see that the instructions were given to anoint the tabernacle and everything that was in it—that means all the furniture, everything that's in the tabernacle, is anointed, and then it becomes a holy place:

"Take the anointing oil and anoint the tabernacle and everything in it; consecrate it and all its furnishings, and it will be holy.

So then, if we look at Leviticus 8:10 once again, it talks about anointing everything that is in the tabernacle so that they may be consecrated:

Then Moses took the anointing oil and anointed the tabernacle and everything in it, and so consecrated them.

The verse says that Moses took up the anointing oil and anointed the tabernacle and everything that was in it. I just want to share at least those two verses with you to show that it goes along the same lines, but there are many more examples in the Old Testament that follow these same chapters and verses when it comes to anointing and concentrating a person, place, or thing.

So, if we are anointing or dressing a person, how exactly do we do that? I am by no means saying that my way is the right way or the only way. I'm simply telling you how I was taught to dress up a person and also how to dress the doors of my home. I'm sure if you asked fifty different workers you would get fifty different answers. But since I'm the one writing this, I am going to tell you how I was taught to do it. And, like I said, this is not the only way, and it is not written in stone.

I was taught that when you dress someone after a cleansing or a spiritual bath that you should dress the crown of their head, the forehead where the third eye would be, the back of the neck between the shoulder blades, over the heart, the crease in both elbows, behind both knees, and the bottoms of both feet. If you are drawing something into you, then you dress the bottoms of the feet from toe to heel. If you are removing something away from you, then you dress the bottoms of the feet from heel to toe. This should be done by making a cross with the oil on all the parts that you are dressing.

Making Your Own Oils

Now it's time to see how to make your own oil. I'm going to share both ways that I have learned over the years. Both ways work with dried roots and herbs. First is the way that I learned to make my spiritual oils back in the seventies. I have since learned another way to make them, and I'm going to share that with you also. Then you can decide which way you like best if you choose to make your own spiritual oils.

Original Blessing Oil Recipe

To make the first type of oil, which is the very first oil I learned to make, you need a double boiler, a large mason jar, olive oil, a white candle, a glass of water, and whatever roots and herbs you are going to put into the oil.

Note: If you grow your own herbs, then you will need to dry them first, and the best way to do that is to pull the roots in the whole plant up. Tie a cotton string around the bottom, and hang it upside down. By doing this, you are letting all the power of that plant go from the roots down into the plant. Just leave them hanging until they're dry.

Then they're ready to use. You need to make sure that they're dried well, because if you don't and you try to put them in a container to keep them in, they will mold. So they need to be completely dried.

When you have all your items laid out, you need to fill the pot with water. Put the other container in the pot and bring it to a boil. While the water is getting hot, add your oil to the mason jar and then set it inside the double boiler.

Once you get the jar in the double boiler, you need to light your candle and say your prayers and petitions over the oil three times. I've added a Bible verse for you to pray over your oil, which will make that oil a protection oil. You don't have to use this prayer if you have one of your own to pray.

2 Samuel 22:3

my God is my rock, in whom I take refuge,
my shield and the horn of my salvation.
He is my stronghold, my refuge and my savior—
from violent people you save me.

After you say your prayer over your oil that you now have heating up, you will also need to say the prayer over your roots and herbs three times before you add them to the oil. You will also need to blow three breaths over the roots and herbs after you say your prayer over them. Then you add them to the oil.

When the water begins to come to a hard boil, lower the heat and let the water simmer until the oil becomes warm. While the oil is in the double boiler, say your prayer over it again three more times. Once the oil becomes warm, then you can turn the fire off, put a lid on the mason jar, and just let it sit in the water until the water cools.

Then you put the jar in a cool place and you repeat the process eight more times. Which means you will be reheating the oil eight more days in a row. You repeat the same process: you say your prayers over the oil. Remember to remove the lid off the mason jar before you add it to the double boiler every time you work the oil.

When the nine days are up, the oil is ready to be used. You can leave the oil in the master jar and just put what you need to work with in a small bottle.

Updated Blessing Oil Recipe

The next oil you can make for yourself is a blessing oil. For this oil you can work with one of the other oils that I shared earlier, or you can make this out of sunflower oil.

You are going to need a large mason jar, the roots and herbs of your choice, sunflower oil, four white stick candles, a white handkerchief, and anything else you might want to add to the oil. You also need a glass of cool water. Lay your white handkerchief out on the table. Pour your oil into the mason jar. Then pray Genesis 49:26 over the oil:

> Your father's blessings are greater
> > than the blessings of the ancient mountains,
> > than the bounty of the age-old hills.
> Let all these rest on the head of Joseph,
> > on the brow of the prince among his brothers.

Then blow three breaths into the oil. Pick up each one of your herbs and say your prayer and petition over each one of them three times. Then blow three breaths over each one of them, and place them in the oil one at a time. Once everything is together, you are going to go back and repeat Genesis 49:26 and also your personal prayer over the jar three times.

Once you have done the prayers, pick up each of the candles one at a time and say your prayer and your petition over each candle. Then you are going to blow three breaths over the candle.

As you do each candle, you are going to place them in a cross candle setup. So the first candle will be put at the top of the jar. The second candle will be placed at the bottom of the jar. The third candle will be placed to the left. And the last candle will be placed to the right.

You light the candles exactly like you set them up. Once the candles are lit, then you will once again say your prayers and petitions over this setup three times.

As the candles burn, you will come back and repeat your prayer and petition another two times. This way you are saying your prayer and petition over the oil three times while the candles burn.

Repeat this process for nine days. Each day you will do your candle setup and you will say your prayers and your petitions over the oil. Once the candles burn out every day, you take the oil and put it in a cool, dark place until the next day when it's time to say your prayers over the oil again.

So there you have it. Two ways to make your own anointing oil. I wanted to share both ways that I make my oils to give you a choice. And once again I am going to shamelessly advise you to get my book *Hoodoo Herbal*, because I feel like it is one of the best ones out there and it has different recipes and a great explanation about roots, herbs, and oils.

16

Baths and Washes

Water is a very powerful source to work with in Conjure. Before we get into the baths and the washes, I want to talk a little bit about the different types of water that can be worked with when you are making baths and washes. Like all things in Conjure, you really need to understand what a thing does—whether it is a root, an herb, an animal bone, or water that you will use to make a bath or a wash.

Water Sources

Not all washes and baths are made with tap water; some are made with water that is collected from different sources. It depends on the work you are doing and your preferences. There are many different water sources that can be worked with in Conjure. I think that it's important that you understand what the different water sources are and where to find them.

When you gather water in its element, it's very powerful, and different types of waters do different types of things in Conjure. I feel like it's important for you to know what the different water sources do in order to be a strong Conjure worker. You also need to know which kinds of water are worked with for what, because you wouldn't want to compromise your working or cause more trouble for yourself—say, by gathering storm water and then trying to use that water in a bath for love. What would end up happening there is that instead of love coming in, it's going to be a whole lot of upset going on. If you're going to do this work, you really need to understand the work and the ingredients that go into the work. It's not really as simple as just throwing some things together—you need to know what those ingredients do.

Running water is very powerful, and that covers any waters that have a flow to them, such as river water or running creek water. These types of waters can be worked with to remove conditions or to send out messages to spirit. What you wouldn't want to ever do, though, is put anything that you are trying to draw up to you in running water, because running water is worked with to remove things that are unwanted from our lives or to remove issues that we may be having. Below you will find a list—and this is not a total list—of some of the types of water that I personally work with, as well as some ideas on how to work with them.

Freezer Water

Freezer water is worked with to stop someone or something. Once the water is frozen, nothing is moving.

Let's say that you have a loved one who is cutting up. You can take a photo of them and a little bit of sugar and place them in a zipper bag. Fill the bag with water until it covers the photo. Let all the air out of the bag and place the bag in the freezer. Let the water freeze with the sugar and the photo. This work is done to cool a person's head when they are not acting right, and when you add the sugar to the water and photo you give that person a sweeter disposition. Once again, even though this may seem simple, it works and it works fast. It is great to calm a household down when there is a lot of argument and upset going on within the home. Freezer work can be worked with for a number of different reasons; this is just one example.

Moon Water

Moon water is gathered for its power. The moon makes emotions run high. If you were doing love work, the moon in Venus would be a great time to have water filled with the energies of Venus. I'm a Leo, so when the moon is in Leo I try to set some water out. The water should be left out overnight, under the full moon. Then when I do my baths, I add a little of the water and it adds extra power to whatever I am working on.

There are other times when a Conjure worker might want to collect moon water. During a new moon, when the moon is dark, that's the time when nothing grows! This water can be worked with to stop a target from achieving whatever they are working on. It is also good to work with to stop bad habits.

Then you have the time when the moon is growing, or waxing. This is a great time to collect the water for works like better business and success works because the moon is growing in power.

Ocean Water

As we know, ocean water is salty. Salt is good for cleansing and refreshing the spirit. If you live near the ocean and the weather permits, you should go at least once a month and take a dip. The water can also be collected to bring home to add to spiritual baths.

River Water

River water is one of my favorite waters to work with. It is used to remove unwanted things from you. River water has a current that will take things and carry them far, far away. When you throw something in the water, if it's cleansing or types of work like that, you want it moved away from you—you don't want it to come back up to you. And the current does that.

One of my elders one time said that if you want to get rid of a person and remove them from your life, all you have to do is take their photo, clean yourself off with it, and go throw it in the river. Simple and easy work to rid yourself of a troublesome person.

There are a lot of workings that can be done with the river. You can also do cleansing baths with river water because this type of water is worked with to remove. You simply collect some river water and use that as the base of the bath.

Stagnant Water

Stagnant water is worked with to stop the movement of a target or thing because the water doesn't move—it becomes sour. This type of water is gathered and worked with to cross or block a target. Just remember: if you decide to work with this type of water, you are responsible for your actions, and if the work isn't justified you could get hit with your own work.

Storm Water

Storm water is gathered when there is a powerful storm going on. This could be a hurricane or a thunder and lightning storm. This type of water is worked with to cause destruction. As we know, hurricanes are very destructive, so when you look at the elements of what a hurricane is and what it does, that is the same thing you will be working with if you do a work with this type of water.

Some workers will work with this type of water to get things moved out of the way because that's what a hurricane does—it moves things around. But it also destroys. This is where your prayers and your petitions come in. Let's say that you had a blocked condition that you could not get rid of no matter how many baths you took or how many cleansings you did. This is the time that hurricane water could be worked with in a positive way. Just like the hurricane pushes everything out of the way, the bath should bust through any blocks or cross conditions that are there.

I believe that all storms have spirits that travel within those storms and that the water from them is very powerful to work with. You have to be careful, though. Even though it may seem like simple work, if you don't have your prayers and your petitions right when you are working, you could cross yourself up. Take your time and learn how to work with these types of waters slowly. This is not the type of work that you want to jump into with both feet.

You need to learn how the water feels, that energy that is running through the water you collected. You can work with your pendulum in order to see the difference in the water. Hurricane water is going to have a different feel and is going to move the pendulum differently than just a regular storm water. You really need to learn the difference between different types of storm waters, and the best way to do that is to understand that energy they put out.

Sun Water

For a fire sign like Leo, the sun is a powerful tool to work with. The sun is at its strongest at what the old folks call high noon. This is when the sun is high in the sky. When you are doing Conjure work, you have to look at all the elements of the thing you are working with. The sun is very powerful because it can burn. It gives off so much heat, it can either drain or energize.

We all get in a rut sometimes—we don't want to go anywhere or do anything. Sun water added to a bath can help your energy start to flow better, which in turn means you will feel better and get to moving around.

Spiritual Waters

Spiritual waters are waters that are made for certain spiritual conditions. They are made with herbs and roots to fix a spiritual condition such as a jinx, someone throwing roots at a target, or maybe a blocked condition. The ingredients are boiled and steeped, just like if you were making a cup of tea. Once the ingredients are steeped and strained, other commercial waters such as Florida Water may be added.

Florida Water

Florida Water is worked with for cooling a hot head. Because it is a cologne and contains alcohol, it is highly flammable and is used in preparing some spiritual items such as railroad spikes. It can also be added to blue water for the protection of a reader who is doing a consultation. Some folks work with it to pull spirit down or to cleanse an area so the spirit will leave after a service; it has many different uses. These days you can even get Florida Water in the grocery store or drugstore.

Holy Water

Holy water can be worked with for cooling one's head just like Florida Water. It is also worked with to remove crossed conditions and to draw in peace and blessings.

Working with Waters

A bath and a wash are basically the same thing; one you can add to the bathwater, the other one you wash everything down with it. They are both made the same way: You collect the ingredients, you put water to boil, you add your ingredients, you say your prayers, and once the water comes to a strong boil you turn the fire off, cover it up, and let it steep. When it's cooled down, the bath or the wash is ready.

Cleansing Bath Basics

Now that we've talked about the different types of water and how they can be worked with, I want to share a few recipes so you get an idea of how to put the waters to work. The first one we're going to look at is a cleansing bath. Even though I have touched on the steps you take when you are starting to do this work, I want to touch on them again because they are important.

Prayer is one of the most important steps to having a successful bath or wash. The prayer and the petition you say over the ingredients depends on what it is that this wash or bath is supposed to do. I'm going to give you a couple of different Bible verses that you can work with when you are making your washes or bath.

Here are the steps that you would do in order to make your bath or your wash. The first thing you need to do is gather all your ingredients. You need a white candle, a glass of water, and whatever roots and herbs that you are adding to the wash.

Once you have everything together, light your candle and say three Our Fathers, three Hail Marys, and three Apostles' Creeds, along with your own personal prayer.

Once you have this done, for all positive baths and washes, it's time to move on and pray Genesis 1:1-11:

1 In the beginning God created the heavens and the earth. 2 Now the earth was formless and empty, darkness was over the surface of the deep, and the Spirit of God was hovering over the waters.

3 And God said, "Let there be light," and there was light. 4 God saw that the light was good, and he separated the light from the darkness. 5 God called the light "day," and the darkness he called "night." And there was evening, and there was morning—the first day.

6 And God said, "Let there be a vault between the waters to separate water from water." 7 So God made the vault and separated the water under the vault from the water above it. And it was so. 8 God called the vault "sky." And there was evening, and there was morning—the second day.

9 And God said, "Let the water under the sky be gathered to one place, and let dry ground appear." And it was so. 10 God called the dry ground "land," and the gathered waters he called "seas." And God saw that it was good.

11 Then God said, "Let the land produce vegetation: seed-bearing plants and trees on the land that bear fruit with seed in it, according to their various kinds." And it was so.

You will then pick up each ingredient and pray the Bible verse over the ingredient. Then add the ingredients to a pot of water. When the water comes to a boil, turn the fire off and steep the ingredients like you would tea.

Once the wash has cooled, it is ready to be strained and used in either a bath or a wash.

Below you will find a few recipes to help you. These are basic recipes that I have used over the last forty-five-plus years.

Simple Cleansing Bath
4 tablespoons salt
4 tablespoons baking soda
4 tablespoons Epsom salt

Each ingredient needs to be prayed over. Then add the ingredients to a pot of boiling water, remove from the heat, and let it cool. While it is cooling, it should be prayed over at least three times before it is added to the bath.

Coffee Bath or Wash
4 tablespoons table salt
1 lemon, halved
1 cup strong black coffee

Make a strong cup of black coffee, and add 4 tablespoons of table salt. Squeeze one whole lemon into the coffee. Use mixture as either a bath or wash. Black coffee is worked with in a bath because it strips away all types of crossed conditions.

To Remove Gossip

Some folks love to gossip. That's their favorite thing to do. And you don't have to do anything to them—most of the time, what they don't know, they make up; and what they do know, they add to it. Gossip is one of the most hurtful things a person can do to another person. If you find yourself being gossiped about, you can take a bath with river water, basil, lemon, and Epsom salt. But before you add the Epsom salt to the other ingredients, you need to hold it in your hand up close to your mouth and pray Proverbs 6:16-19 over the salt three times:

16 There are six things the LORD hates,
seven that are detestable to him:

17 haughty eyes,
a lying tongue,
hands that shed innocent blood,

18 a heart that devises wicked schemes,
feet that are quick to rush into evil,

19 a false witness who pours out lies
and a person who stirs up conflict in the community.

This wash is also good to clean your home with if you have a lot of folks who are sticking their nose in your business and talking about your family life. To use the wash, you would clean the house from back to front. Make sure you wash all the doors inside and out and also wipe the windows down.

I hope you have a better understanding of working with the different types of waters and also how to work with their power. Water is a powerful thing. It can not only cleanse but also destroy. Just be mindful of the works that you do, and make sure that you do some type of divination before doing any type of work—even cleansing work. You might not need to do a cleansing—you might need to do some other type of work to help your situation. That's why divination is a must before you start reaching for roots and herbs and doing all these kinds of different work. Use your common sense and get your skills together when doing this work. Even though the work seems to be so simple, it is still magic.

17

Dirts and Powders

Dirt is one of my favorite tools to work with, because it picks up the spirit of the land and it holds that spirit within itself. It's a very powerful tool, and it doesn't cost anything to gather it except for your appreciation and thanks.

When I was coming up as a young Rootworker, dirts and powders were an important part of my lessons. In the old days, powders and dirts were worked with a lot, because you could trick them and then go directly to the target's home and drop them, and no one would ever be the wiser. I don't think that a lot of folks nowadays realize how important powders and dirts from different locations really are and how powerful they are.

I think that in today's world, the making of powders has been so commercialized that new folks coming in think that that's the norm. When I was coming up as a young worker, I was taught that powders are made from dirts from different locations and also from powdered herbs. Sometimes chalk would be added to the powder, depending on what the powder was for.

In today's world, most powders are nothing more than colored talc. You don't have to pound the herbs anymore, because we have so many electronics nowadays that can just turn it into a fine powder with the flip of a switch. Of course, the old way is always better, but it's a busy day and age and you have to work with what you have. Some roots and herbs are hard to powder when you're doing them by hand, so it only makes sense to use something that is going to get the job done faster. Although I do think using electronics changes the feel of the herbs and roots. I don't know if it's because it's run by electricity or if it's because we are not manually doing the grinding and powdering. I think that doing it electrically removes the power and the focus that we put into powdering the roots and herbs by hand. We have to remember that like begets like. We draw what we are, and the energy you put into an herb powdering it by hand is a powerful thing.

Dirts

Dirts from different areas and different kinds of dirt do different things. I've written about the types of different dirts, but I don't think that I have ever gone into any true detail that truly explains exactly what some dirts do and how to turn them into powders. I want to really go into detail with it here because I feel like this is a part of Conjure that is dying out as the elders die off. And I think that it's because folks don't really know how to work with the dirts and powders, much less how to make them. So I want to touch on different situations where different elements of dirt can be worked with.

Ant Mound Dirt

Let's start with ants. Ants are those funny little animals that run from place to place and they can travel a long distance. Ants are workers. When you do this type of work, you have to look at whatever you are working with—what its purpose is and also what it does. We know that ants gather in communities. We also know that they bite. And we know from watching them that they are workers. They will work their little fingers to the bone for the bed that is their home. So if we understand what the ant's nature really is, then we should know that the dirt from an ant mound can be worked with to move someone out of the way without harming them, without causing them to wander for the rest of their life, like hotfoot powder does, which we'll get to in a minute.

I'm going to give you a couple of different works that can be worked using ant mound dirt.

TO REMOVE A TARGET

I have used this first work often over the last fifty years. For those sensitive to the suffering of insects and the like, I feel like I need to say this: Conjure work is not all sweet and sugary. If you have an issue or are not comfortable with closing ants up in a jar, don't do this work. I'm of a mind that just because you *know* how to do something doesn't mean that you *have* to do it. You and you alone are responsible for the things that you do and don't do.

To start, gather some ant mound dirt along with the ants and place them in a glass jar with a lid on it. Leave the ants in the jar until they stop moving. I have seen it take a few days for this to happen.

Once the ants stop moving, take some of the dirt out of the jar. (You can save the rest for later date. It's never going to go bad.)

You can either take a photo of the target and burn it to ash, or you can write their name and address on a piece of paper and burn that to ash. Then you mix that with the dirt from the ant mound while praying that the target move out.

If you are not sure of what to pray over the dirt, you can pray Zechariah 14:4:

> On that day his feet will stand on the Mount of Olives, east
> of Jerusalem, and the Mount of Olives will be split in two
> from east to west, forming a great valley, with half of the
> mountain moving north and half moving south.

So, when praying there, you are giving spirit the option to take your target anywhere—north, east, south, or west, as long as they are moving away from you. You can also burn the Bible verse into ash and mix it with the ant dirt.

When you say a prayer over something, it needs to be done in threes. Three represents God the Father, God the Son, and God the Holy Spirit, which make up the Holy Trinity. Three is a very powerful number. Once you have your dirt (or should say powder, because it has now become a powder), it's moved from just being ant dirt to being a working powder that you can drop in the path of the target to get them moving.

When you are ready to deploy your powder, you can literally go to where the target works, where they live, where they eat at normally, and drop the powder. The important thing is that they get into the powder. The easiest way to do this is to simply go where they are and drop the powder across the doorway. Folks are not even going to know what it is because it looks like dirt and we track dirt in and out all day long. It is easy to make up a powder and then go to someone's home and sprinkle that powder on the way going in and dropping it inside their home, and they will never know it, because it just looks like dirt. That's why this work is called tricks, because you are laying the trick down. This can also be done with oils—you simply have to know what you are doing.

If the target lives with you and you are trying to get them to move out into their own place, then all you have to do is dress their shoes. Lift the soles of their shoes up and sprinkle some of the powder in there. Replace the soles and just go on about your business.

Don't stay focused on the work, wondering if it's going to work or it's not going to work or whatever. You did the job, now go on about your business and forget about it and let spirit take control. Because if we keep worrying about a job that we've done, that is telling spirit that we do not trust them to do what we've prayed for and petitioned to happen.

So we looked at working with an ant bed to move someone out. But what about working with it to make something happen in a hurry?

TO HURRY THINGS ALONG

Ant mound dirt can be worked with when you are doing a court case work and it seems like it is taking forever for the case to get over with. I'm going to explain to you why this works, because you may be thinking, *What in the world? How does ant mound dirt work with a court case?* When you gather the dirt, it can't be helped that you close those ants up with that dirt. I mean, you're going to catch some ants even if you tried not to. All you're going to do is get bitten if you try not to include the ants with the dirt. They're going to eat you up. So when you're gathering that dirt and you get those ants in that jar and you put the lid on that jar, those ants are going to try their best to get out of that jar. They're going to work hard. They're going to move around fast, and they're going to do everything that they can do to get out of that situation that they're in. They are putting forth a lot of energy and work to get out of there as fast as they can. That energy is what is going to help your work.

I'm going to share with you a Bible verse that you can work with when dealing with court casework—it is my go-to when I am working for someone to try and help them not to be incarcerated.

STAYING OUT OF JAIL

I have worked with this next Bible verse over the years for my clients who have gotten into something and are trying to stay out of jail. This is a work that one of my elders gave me many years ago. It can be done in many different ways, but I'm going to give you a simple but powerful way to do the work.

We're going to look at Genesis 19:15:

With the coming of dawn, the angels urged Lot, saying,
"Hurry! Take your wife and your two daughters who are
here, or you will be swept away when the city is punished."

It tells us that the angels are speaking to Lot, telling him to get up and to *move fast* or he could be consumed in the punishment that God has for the city. This working will similarly help move things along quickly.

For this working, you need a photo of the person you are working for, a glass bowl, a pair of real handcuffs with the key, some dirt from the front and back of the house that the person lives in, the dirt from your ant bed that you have prepared, a white nine-day candle, sugar, and copies of your court paperwork. You also need to print out or tear right out of the Bible Genesis 19:15.

(Before some of y'all get up in arms because I said tear it right out of the Bible, if you know your Bible, and you know God's word, then you know that the word of God cannot be burnt. Try it for yourself. You're still going to be able to see the words in the ash. That is what makes it so powerful.)

When you have all your ingredients together, sit down at the table. Of course, you are going to say your prayers before you are going to start this work. Light the candle and say three God the Fathers, three Hail Marys, and three Apostles' Creeds (these are in the back of the book).

Then you are going to pray Genesis 19:15 over the candle and pray your petition over the candle three times.

Once this is done, you are ready to put together your work. You need to pray over every ingredient. Start with the person's photo that you are working for, then the Bible verse, then burn them to ash. Just drop them in a fireproof container and let them burn. Now you add the dirt from the front and back door, then pour the sugar over the dirt, photo, and Bible verse. You use sugar because sugar runs fast. You wouldn't want to put something that runs slow even though it's sweet in this work because you need fast action. For example, molasses is something sweet that runs slow. It pours slowly, so it is worked in works to slow a target down. It is an offering given to St. Martha the Dominator. St Martha the Dominator is very powerful when it comes to protection and justice work.

Once you have all the ingredients in the bowl, you take the handcuffs and open them up as far as they will open. Lay them in the bowl where each end is not touching. Then set your candle in the bowl on top of the sugar. Make sure—and this is important—that you remove the key to the handcuffs completely away from the work. Take it and put it in another room somewhere. Don't lose that key, though, because you can cleanse those handcuffs after this job and reuse them in other works.

It is important that you pray over this work three times a day and you say your prayers three times. I can't stress how powerful the number three is.

Bank Dirt

Another dirt that I want to bring to your attention is the dirt from a bank. As we know, banks hold millions of dollars every day. So the dirt from a bank is wonderful for prosperity works, for getting raises at work, and for all types of money work. But there is another side to that coin.

Banks also repossess vehicles, they take away folks' homes, they repossess anything that you owe them money for if you are unable to pay. So therefore, banks not only give but they also take away, and sometimes there's heartache and despair when you're dealing with a bank. I just want you to be mindful and to look at the whole picture of what these institutions do when you work with these dirts.

Graveyard Dirt

I believe that graveyard dirt is like a double-edged sword. It can be worked with for positive reasons and for negative reasons. Also, you have to look at the spirits that roam the graveyard. Not every spirit is a loving, light type of spirit. Some of them were miserable in life and they're still miserable even in death, so just be mindful. Pay attention. Don't just jump into something with two feet.

The graveyard has become a trend. Folks are throwing caution to the wind and just playing in the graveyard. I have even heard of folks sleeping in them. For me, the dead and their home are to be respected. There is a right way to enter and to leave. You should never take visiting a graveyard lightly. Always be very respectful, and you should always ask for permission before you take anything from a grave, be it dirt or something that has been left there. Some items can be worked with, but you should always ask.

It is best to bring a pendulum with you if you are at a graveyard where you have no blood kin buried. Once you find the right grave, you should get to know the spirit buried there. Don't just start asking for dirt. Clean the headstone, just talk to them, bring them some flowers, say some prayers for them. Make a few trips to bond with them. Do divination and work with the pendulum to make sure you are at the right grave. When the time feels right, then you can ask them for help, or some dirt. Maybe even to bury something with them to hold for you.

You cannot rush this getting to know each other phase, or respecting the graveyard. Remember if you take something, you give something in return. You also need to remember that you should pay going in and pay going out of the gates. I keep some coins in my car for this purpose. Once on the outside of the gate, you should brush your feet off and splash some Florida Water on, just to make sure nothing came out of the graveyard with you.

Graveyard dirt can be worked with for many different kinds of conditions. The spirit can be petitioned to go after a target, the spirit can be petitioned to help with any difficult situation—it all depends on what the work is being done for. They are very powerful when it comes to protection and reversals. The most important thing is to be very respectful and to build a bond with the spirit if they are not blood kin. As long as you take care of them, they will take care of you.

Home Dirt

Some of the most powerful dirt that you can work with when you are trying to draw something into your home is the dirt that your home sits on. There is nothing stronger than the spirit of the land that your home sits on. Those spirits are invested in you and your home because you take care of those spirits when you tend to your yard and your home.

Normally, dirt from the four corners of the property and the front and back doors are worked with. When you are trying to nail your house down to keep it safe, you would also include the dirt from the four corners of your home in the work.

SPEEDING THINGS UP

The next work I want to share is to speed something up. This could be the purchase of something, getting a new job, buying a home, selling a home—anything that you need to move fast. I'm just going to give you general instructions on how to do this work, but the same instructions can be adjusted to any job.

If you want to buy a home, you need to get the dirt from that home that is for sale and bring it home. To that dirt you are going to add a large magnet because you are trying to draw this home to you. You will get the photo of the real estate agent who has the home for sale, and you need a red candle because red is hot and works fast. You also need your Bible verse, Genesis 45:13:

> Tell my father about all the honor accorded me in
> Egypt and about everything you have seen. And bring my
> father down here quickly."

Place the dirt that you got from the home that you want to buy in a glass bowl. To that bowl add the real estate agent's photo or name or company that they work for. Burn the Bible verse to ash and then cover it with the sugar. The magnet and the sugar are worked with to draw and sweeten. And of course the Bible verse is prayed over the work to make this happen fast.

You should always say your personal prayers before you start any type of spiritual work. Actually, you should say them daily, at least three times a day, morning, noon, and at night before you go to bed. Just keep working the bowl and keep the candle burning until you see success.

A few words of advice are needed here, I feel. Do not choose a home or a job or a vehicle, whatever it may be, that you are not qualified for. Always work on something that is in your area of expertise or financial ability. If you want a million-dollar home and you only make $50,000 a year, that's going to be kind of out of your reach. Work toward the things that you can achieve and grow from there. I am in no way saying that a million-dollar home is not possible; what I'm saying is that you have to be reasonable and work with what you have. If you want a million-dollar home, then put in the work and work toward it and achieve that dream. It can be done. Dreams do come true. But you have to put the work in in order to make that happen. Nothing is free in this life. Everything costs something.

Sand

The next dirt that I want to share is actually sand, because it comes from the beach. This sand is kind of like a double-action work, because you can work with the sand to draw someone or something in or you can work with it to remove something or someone. This is because you have the ebb and flow of the beach water. The water comes in and draws things in, and then the water goes back out and takes things away.

I only work with this sand for one condition at a time. I know some folks believe that you can throw something out in the ocean and the waves are going to take it away, which they do, but they also bring that thing back. The only time I do that kind of work is if I'm trying to punish a target: so when the waves take the work out they have peace; but then when the waves bring the work back in, they get hit with the work again because that is exactly what happens if you throw a work out in the ocean.

I know some workers will do this with love work, that is, throw something in the ocean, and it's never made sense to me. My common sense tells me that what's going to happen is when the work is coming in, my lover is going to be there with me and be solid, but when the work is taken out, then they are going to become flaky and undependable. I'm just using this as an example so you can see how working with the beach and ocean could affect the work. But if you work with the sand itself, that's a different story.

If you are trying to draw something to you, then when the beach water comes in, dig you up a handful of sand. If you are trying to remove something from you and you want to work with the elements of the beach, then when the water goes out, get your dirts because it's going to hold those energies. When you are doing this work and you are working with dirts, animals, herbs, roots, prayers, you have to look at the whole picture and you need to use your common sense. The beach is a very powerful place in itself, and anything that comes out of it holds that power.

Termite Dirt

The next dirt that I want to share some information about is termite dirt. Once again, you're going to look at the animal. What exactly do termites do? Termites will eat wood until there is nothing left, and then what happens is they destroy the foundation of the home. Termite dirt is not as hard to get as you might think—that is, there are a lot of old buildings and old places out in this world. You could just do a walk-through and find termites and their dust that they leave behind from eating up the wood that they destroy.

So what exactly does the termite do besides just eating wood? One, they work fast; they can destroy a piece of wood in no time. Two, they destroy everything. And three, they are hard to get rid of. So, if you were trying to get rid of an enemy, then termite dust, dark wood, whatever it is that you can find to work with, is ideal because of the conditions that termites cause; the same conditions can be worked with to remove an enemy from your life. That energy is in the dust or the wood that the termite leaves behind. Termites do not work alone—there's a whole colony, which is why they are able to destroy so much so fast. So therefore, whatever they are destroying picks up that energy of all those worker termites, so it's perfect to destroy a target. Like I said, some of the works that are done in Conjure are dark. But if you're realistic, you cannot have light without dark. And life is not all sugary sweet.

A NOTE OF CAUTION

I want to touch on this before I go further: When you are gathering dirt to work with, you have to understand that the dark could be like a double-edged sword. Maybe a dirt is meant to destroy a target. But if you are not careful, that dirt might harm you instead. Here's an instance: Hospital dirt is worked with to heal, and yet there are times when a person can't be healed and they pass away. So if we believe that a place holds a spirit, we have to believe that hospital dirt not only has a healing power but it also holds the power of sadness, misery, and tears. I just want to bring a few examples to your attention so you understand how important it is when you work with these dirts that your prayers and petitions are straight to the point. Be very clear with your petition on what it is that you are trying to achieve when you work with these different types of dirt.

I'm trying to save you from making some of the mistakes that I made as a young worker. Use your common sense. Look at the whole picture, look at the positive and the negative. Don't rush your work. Take your time. There are fifty different works that you can do for the same situation, for the same case, and none of them will be the same. So when you're deciding that you need to do a job, make sure that you think it through. Pray on it. Do divination on it. Petition the spirits to help you discern what is the right way to do the job so it will be a success.

Other Dirts

I just want to touch on some of the other different kinds of dirt that can be worked with just to give you an idea of what these dirts can do to help empower your work. Below you will find some different dirts and I will explain what they are worked for.

> **Church dirt** can be worked with for repairing family issues, drawing in blessings, for healing and protection works, and also peaceful home types of work.

> **Courthouse dirt** is worked with for court cases to bring forth justice, drawing the law to a target, and to keep the law away from your home.

Crossroads dirt is good to work with if you are opening the roads, drawing in blessings, nailing something down, or trying to get a new skill.

Dirt from fighting dogs is good dirt to have if you can get your hands on some dirt from a yard where dogs have been fighting. You can even get this dirt from a dog park where dogs will have been scuffling with each other. This dirt can be worked with to cause confusion or to cause two targets to fight and argue. It is also worked with to cause destruction.

Police station dirt can either be worked with to draw the law to a target or to keep the law away.

Railroad track dirt is worked with for power to draw something to you and also to remove something away from you.

River dirt is good for making a dolly that is worked for cleansing work. It is also good for removing someone or something away from you.

Powders

Hotfoot Powder

I feel like hotfoot powder is what everyone goes to when they're trying to move someone out of the way, which is most of the time unethical to work with. I'm going to tell you why most folks don't understand that hotfoot work does more than just removing a target from where you don't want them to be. Hotfoot powder contains graveyard dirt in it. Anyone who has worked with the spirits of the dead know that they are relentless. They don't give up. So when you add that graveyard dirt into the powder, and you're adding all these other things in that powder, it actually causes the target to never be at peace.

Old-school workers understand this, and that's why hotfoot powder is a last resort. It should be put right up there with burying a target in the graveyard. You truly can ruin someone's life with hotfoot powder. You could cause the target to never be settled in a job, to never be settled in a relationship, to never be settled in one state. This is why divination is so important before you do any type of work.

What you don't realize is that any work that is done can be undone, and it can be sent back your way. Energy is always going to go where it came from. You need to always remember that. I have been doing this work for a long time, and I've seen a lot of things. I have seen workers who have done unethical things, and those things, those works, those jobs have come back on them. When it comes back to them, they are quick to say that someone is throwing at them, someone is cursing them, someone has put a crossed condition on them. No. What has happened is they decided that this work was justified without checking into it first, and their actions caught up to them. In truth, they did it to themselves. Because at the end of every day, when we work on someone, if it's unjustified and they know enough to get that work off of them, they are going to send that work right back where it came from once again, because energy is going to go where it started at.

I don't mean to sound preachy. I'm just trying to get the facts across so maybe it will save a few people reading this a whole lot of trouble and heartache. If you just do divination before you do any type of work, it'll save you a whole lot of lessons. I'm speaking from experience. The old folks say, "A hard head makes a soft behind." Well, when I was coming up, I didn't always do divination before I did a work, and I learned the hard way. The path of least resistance is always the better path to take. If you want to move someone out of the way, instead of jumping in with both feet and hotfooting them, try one of the earlier works in this chapter with ant hill dirt.

Sulfur

Sulfur is worked with to clear a home or place out where there are unruly spirits. A pinch of sulfur behind the door of the home will protect against cross conditions and false friends.

Sulfur is well known for driving out unwanted spirits. It is said that carrying a little sulfur and salt in a Conjure bag on your person will keep the plat-eye away. Growing up, we were told stories of the plat-eye. If we told a lie, my mama would call us on it and say, "You lying like a plat-eye!" It was hard to keep anything from my mama, and she let us know it. The plat-eye is basically a demon or evil spirit that can shapeshift. It can be found anywhere where someone died a horrible death. It is a trickster spirit, and it's said that when it gets on you that you change. It's also a lying spirit, and with every lie you tell, it grows bigger and bigger and its eyes glow redder and redder. After a while, you don't know the difference between the truth and a lie!

Vesta Powder

If you think you've been crossed, you can do a cleansing with some vesta powder. Vesta powder is made from saltpeter (potassium nitrate) and cornmeal. It's very volatile and has been known to cause fires. It will clear out whatever is there. You can make your own, or you can buy it from a shop. If you have never worked with vesta powder, I would advise you to hire someone to come and clear the home for you. It takes very little of the powder to clear out a home; it is one of those things where a little is enough. Use caution when doing cleansing around the home. Potassium nitrate is toxic; wear gloves if you're handling it yourself.

Making Your Own Powders

If you decide to make your own powders, then you need to gather the dirts for the different condition powders, powder your herbs and roots, and then mix them along with the dirt. I'm not saying that you shouldn't add a base powder. A base powder is good when you are making a powder that you are going to wear—it makes the powder feel better on the skin. But traditionally powders are made from dirts and powdered roots and herbs. Burning things to ash also helps to empower the powder that you are making and it also links the target to that powder. As a worker you will have to decide how you make your products and what goes into them. I am simply trying to give you different options and the traditional way that powders are made.

And remember, you and you alone are responsible for the works that you do. You should always do a divination on a situation before you do any type of magical workings on it. You should train yourself now and get into the habit of divining on a situation before you act on it. I don't do any type of work without divination, and if spirit says not to do the work, you should not to do it because you don't know what that action could cause, and you have to remember that every action causes a reaction. You wouldn't want to get hit with your own work because you did work that was unjustified. There aren't a whole lot of rules and regulations to this work, but justification is a big one and that is one rule that I do not play around with. I'm speaking from experience here. When you're a young worker, you do all kinds of works that you feel you're entitled to do—but sometimes those works will bite you in the behind if they were unjustified.

18

Candle Work

I was not raised up burning candles except for the emergency candles when electric would go out. When I was young, my aunt took me to the Catholic church without my mama knowing it. My mama had a total meltdown when she found out, but I was hooked. I loved the whole experience, and I knew my life was going to change because, believe it or not, I fainted in church during mass. So I didn't have a choice but to tell my mama that I had gone to the Catholic church for mass. When I left home at seventeen, I became a Catholic. All my children and grand-children are baptized in the Catholic church. Of course, my mama didn't approve, but she really didn't say anything negative about it once she saw how serious I was.

I love working with candles—the feel of the wax, the flame mov-ing as you say your prayers over the candle. My fourth grade teacher, Mrs. Hall, taught us how to make candles in her class. She also taught us how to crochet. Even after all these years I can still close my eyes and see her. That is the impact that she had on me. She reinforced my mama's teachings that you could do anything and be anything that you wanted to as long as you believed in yourself and did the work. That was really my very first experience with wax and candles. We made the candles out of the old gulf wax, and we colored them with broken crayons.

For many years I made my own candles that way. Candles, eggs, and then washes were the first tools I learned to work with at seventeen years old. Since then, my skills and candle making have become much better, because I now make my candles in molds instead of hand dipping them. Candle wax holds a memory, so when you say your prayers and breathe your breath over that wax, the wax latches on and holds that energy. Then, when you light the candle, the flame sends your prayers and petitions out to spirit.

Some of the best advice that I can give you is to not work with wax or candles when you are upset because the wax will pick up that energy that you are putting off. When we are upset, we can't think clearly because we are so focused on the issue. So the best thing to do is to clear your head and then do your work. You are responsible for every work you do. You wouldn't want to do something when you are angry and then be sorry for it later, so always try to work with a cool head.

Nowadays, there are many different types of candles, many different shapes and sizes—but I want to share with you how to work with a stick candle the old way, the way I was first taught, so that's what we're going to look at. I am going to touch on different types of candles a little bit, but as far as doing magic with candles, I want to talk about working with stick candles and being able to make your own stick candles. I want to give you directions on how to make them.

When you make your own candles, that is a power that you cannot buy, because as you are making the candle you have all your focus on the prayers and the petitions that you are saying over that wax.

Candle Colors

Before we get into the making of the candle itself, though, I want to talk a little bit about the different colors of candles and how the color affects the outcome of the burn. This is the way I work with the candles and their colors. I am by no means saying it is the only way, or that everyone else works with these same colors for the same thing when they are burning candles. This is just my way.

> **Red candles** are worked with when you want to draw something to you. They are burned in attraction work, love work, or any type of work that you are trying to heat up. They are

also burned in works of Shut Your Mouth and Run Devil Run. The color red is hot, so any types of work that you need to heat up or you need to be hot you could burn a red candle.

Orange candles can be burned for power, domination, control, blockbusting, attraction work, better business, road opening, crown of success, and boss fix. Orange is made with red and yellow: red is a hot color and yellow is a power color, so when you mix the two together to make orange you have a color that is very powerful.

Green candles can be worked with for money, prosperity, good luck, and sometimes healing work because the color green can represent the earth. And we know that the earth and the land absorb things.

Blue candles are one of my favorites to work with for money and prosperity. They seem to work well for me. They are also good to work with for a peaceful home, healing, wisdom, and sometimes extra power when they are burned beside another candle.

Purple candles are very powerful. I had an elder one time tell me not to ever burn three purple candles in a straight line because it is dangerous. She didn't really go into a lot of detail about it, but I took her at her word. Purple can be worked with for power, domination, control, Do as I Say, mastery over an enemy, and many other works.

Black candles I feel like have been given a bad name, a bad reputation. A lot of the young workers that I have come across seem to have a fear of burning black candles. As a young worker myself, I was taught that burning white candles was actually more dangerous than burning black ones. As we know, if you have ever worn a black shirt outside in the summertime, the heat from the sun just bears down on you and that black absorbs the heat. So therefore our common sense should tell us that black candles will absorb the prayers, the cleansing, and hold on to the work. Black candles are great for cleansing work, for reversal works, and also when you are doing enemy work and your petition is that the enemy be held down and kept away from you.

White candles hold all colors because all candles start as white wax before color wax chips are added to them. When I was a young worker back in the 70s, there weren't a lot of different candle colors to work with unless you made your own candles. As a young worker, I was taught that white candles are more powerful than black candles because, as we know, black candles pull things off of you. I was taught that a white candle can do everything you need it to do. Some ole folks even say it can kill a target. In my old age, I have gone back to working with either white or Black candles depending on what I am working on. If you don't have the color candle you need, then just work with a white one.

Making Your Own Candles

Once you decide what condition the work is going to be done for, then you need to gather up all your supplies. To make your own candles, you need wax, wax coloring chips, or you could just use wax crayons like I did when I first started making candles. You also need a double boiler to melt the wax in, and some wicking. (When I first started making candles, I melted the wax in a tin can in a pot of water. That was my double boiler. Use what you have on hand. Don't go out and buy a bunch of candle making supplies.)

You are going to be making a hand-dipped candle. You need to cut your wick to the length you want your candle to be plus about three extra inches because you have to hold on to the wick as you dip the candle into the wax.

Once you have everything together, place your wax in the double boiler. Be mindful of how hot the wax gets because it can put off poisonous vapors if you get it too hot. Also, if the wax is too hot, it will not stick to the wick; it will just pull the wax off of the wick.

Once you get your wax melted, you can either burn the Bible verse to ash or you can just drop the Bible verse down into the bottom of the wax. Make sure that you have a copy of the Bible verse, though, because you are going to need to pray that Bible verse along with your petition as you build your candle. You could also burn your prayer and petition to ash and drop it in the wax, so that with every dip of that wick, you pick up the power of that petition and prayer that is infused in the wax and also the prayer and petition that you are praying over the wax as you build your candle. This is a little trick that an elder shared with me a long time ago and I've never forgotten it; when I make these types of stick candles I usually burn my Bible verse and my petition and add the ash to the wax. By doing this, you are adding more power to your candle.

When the wax is ready, take the wick and dip it in the wax. This is tedious work, but it is well worth it. When you first start dipping the wick in the wax, it seems like it is going to take forever, but it really doesn't. It may look like there's no wax on the wick unless you use a dark-colored wax, but trust me, there is wax on that wick.

Mash the wax into the wick, and repeat this process until you can really see the wax on there. Once the wax has got a good hold of the wick, then you just dip the wick in the wax continuously. Give each dipping time to dry before you dip again. Keep praying over the wax and the candle as you work.

Below are some Bible verses that will help with different situations. You can work with these verses when you are making your candles.

For victory:

Numbers 10:9

When you go into battle in your own land against an enemy who is oppressing you, sound a blast on the trumpets. Then you will be remembered by the Lord your God and rescued from your enemies.

For protection:

Proverbs 1:30-33

30 Since they would not accept my advice
   and spurned my rebuke,

31 they will eat the fruit of their ways
   and be filled with the fruit of their schemes.

32 For the waywardness of the simple will kill them,
   and the complacency of fools will destroy them;

33 but whoever listens to me will live in safety
   and be at ease, without fear of harm."

For block busting:

Exodus 3:18-20

18 "The elders of Israel will listen to you. Then you and the elders are to go to the king of Egypt and say to him, 'The Lord, the God of the Hebrews, has met with us. Let us take a three-day journey into the wilderness to offer sacrifices to the Lord our God.' 19 But I know that the king of Egypt will not let you go unless a mighty hand compels him. 20 So I will stretch out my hand and strike the Egyptians with all the wonders that I will perform among them. After that, he will let you go.

For prosperity:

Deuteronomy 28:11

The Lord will grant you abundant prosperity—in the fruit of your womb, the young of your livestock and the crops of your ground—in the land he swore to your ancestors to give you.

For uncrossing:

Judges 15:10-17

10 The people of Judah asked, "Why have you come to fight us?"
"We have come to take Samson prisoner," they answered, "to do to him as he did to us."

11 Then three thousand men from Judah went down to the cave in the rock of Etam and said to Samson, "Don't you realize that the Philistines are rulers over us? What have you done to us?"

He answered, "I merely did to them what they did to me."

12 They said to him, "We've come to tie you up and hand you over to the Philistines."

Samson said, "Swear to me that you won't kill me yourselves."

13 "Agreed," they answered. "We will only tie you up and hand you over to them. We will not kill you." So they bound him with two new ropes and led him up from the rock. 14 As he approached Lehi, the Philistines came toward him shouting. The Spirit of the Lord came powerfully upon him. The ropes on his arms became like charred flax, and the bindings dropped from his hands. 15 Finding a fresh jawbone of a donkey, he grabbed it and struck down a thousand men.

16 Then Samson said,

"With a donkey's jawbone
  I have made donkeys of them.
With a donkey's jawbone
  I have killed a thousand men."

17 When he finished speaking, he threw away the jawbone; and the place was called Ramath Lehi.

When the candle is the size that you want it to be, put it up somewhere for it to cure for at least twenty-four hours. If you try to burn the candle right after it is made, you're going to waste the candle because it's going to burn too fast.

Once you have your stick candle finished, you can use your pendulum if you work with one to test the power of the candle. If the candle does not move the pendulum like you would like it to move it, then you will need to continue to say your prayers over the candle until it holds the power that you need it to have.

When you are ready to burn your candle, make sure that you blow three breaths on the candle, one breath at a time, and say your prayer and your petition over the candle three times. Your candle is then ready to burn.

Remember to say your other prayers before you start doing your candle work, and also remember to have your glass of water sitting on the altar with your candle. Here's a bit of caution: make sure that you place your candle in a fireproof holder, and do not for any reason leave that candle unattended.

Making your own candles is really better if it's at all possible because you are empowering them with your petitions and your prayers as you are making them. You know exactly the mood you were in when you made them and you know the ingredients that you put into them and the prayers that went into them. There is nothing like doing the work and making your own candles. To me, making candles is very relaxing and I like the feel of the wax. It may seem stressful at first when you are learning, but once you get the hang of it I think you'll like it.

CONCLUSION:
BUILDING A STRONG
FOUNDATION

I didn't learn what I know out of books. I learned at the knee of my elders I have had over the years. The old saying is, "When it's time, the teacher will appear." Sometimes the teacher is only there for a season, and sometimes they are there for a lifetime. The spirits that walk with you always know what you need, and they are always on time.

My mama didn't explain to us what she was doing and why, she just did it, and we watched her because it was part of our everyday life. Like no shoes in the house. We took our shoes off at the door and she would wipe them down with turpentine. This was an everyday routine, it never varied. Then we would take them to our bedrooms. I know it was turpentine because I know the smell; later on in life, one of my elders told me that turpentine was worked with to remove cross conditions. Turpentine will cut away any type of mess, and it can also protect.

When something is part of your everyday life, it becomes a habit, it blends in with your routine that you do daily. Conjure is a part of my everyday life. I live it! It's not just something that I do when I need something. If I removed Conjure from my life, I wouldn't even know how to cook or how to clean my home; I would be lost as a goose without its head. This is the only way I know how to live. It's how I was raised and it's what I know. Things that I have learned over these years I have taught to my children and my grandchildren, not by sitting them down and giving them lessons, but by my actions and answering questions that they have, because that is how they have learned to take care of their homes and their families.

When my mother was alive my older children spent a lot of time with her, so things that she did naturally they have picked up. Here's an example. To this day, I cannot stand Vicks salve. Vicks salve, or camphor, is an old Conjure remedy to remove an ailment that could have possibly been put on you through the evil eye and cause you to become ill with a bad cold. My mama would rub our feet with Vicks salve and make us put on white socks and go to bed. If we had a bad cough, she would make us eat the Vicks to clear out whatever was there. My daughter to this day does this if she gets sick. Did my mama tell her this is the old Conjure remedy to remove a cross condition that's believed to be brought on by the evil eye? No. She just treated her illness with no explanation, and it worked, so my daughter has passed this on to her own children who, every time they get sick, they break out the Vicks! Vicks can be worked with for uncrossing because of the ingredients that are in it. There are a lot of household products that elders have worked with that folks nowadays don't even know about because it's being lost.

I hope that you learn something from this book to put to use and maybe teach someone. Every book I write, that's what I expect and that's what I want, to share the knowledge. The purpose of the book is so folks can learn this work because it is dying out. Every elder that dies, we've lost knowledge that we're never going to be able to get back. All I know is the old ways. This is what I write about and what I teach.

COMMON PRAYERS

Our Father

Our Father, Who art in heaven, hallowed be Thy name. Thy kingdom come; Thy will be done, on earth as it is in heaven. Give us this day our daily bread; and forgive us our trespasses as we forgive those who trespass against us; and lead us not into temptation, but deliver us from evil.

Hail Mary

Hail Mary,
Full of grace,
The Lord is with thee.
Blessed art thou among women,
and blessed is the fruit
of thy womb, Jesus.
Holy Mary,
Mother of God,
pray for us sinners, now
and at the hour of our death.
Amen.
Behold the handmaid of the Lord:
Be it done unto me according to Thy word.

Apostles' Creed

*I believe in God, the Father Almighty, Creator of Heaven
and earth;*

and in Jesus Christ, His only Son, Our Lord,

*Who was conceived by the Holy Ghost, born of the Virgin
Mary, suffered under Pontius Pilate, was crucified, died,
and was buried.*

St. Clare Prayer

*O most Holy Trinity, Father, Son and Holy Spirit, we praise
Thy Holy Name and the wonders of grace Thou hast worked
in Thy servant, St. Clare. Through her powerful inter-
cession grant us the favors we beg in this novena, above
all the grace to live and die as she did in Thy most Holy
Love. Amen.*

Glory Be

*Glory Be to the Father, and to the Son, and to the Holy
Spirit. As it was in the beginning, is now, and ever shall be,
world without end.*

ALSO BY STARR CASAS

Hoodoo Your Love: Conjure the Love You Want (and Keep It)

Hoodoo Herbal: Folk Recipes for Conjure & Spellwork with Herbs, Houseplants, Roots & Oils

Divination Conjure Style: Reading Cards, Throwing Bones, and Other Forms of Household Fortune-Telling

Old Style Conjure: Hoodoo, Rootwork, & Folk Magic

The Conjure Workbook Volume 1: Working the Root

ABOUT THE AUTHOR

STARR CASAS was born in the mountains of Kentucky and raised in the culture of the Deep South, and she continues to hold tight to the folk ways of her ancestors. At the age of seventeen, Starr learned how to do cleansings with eggs, herbs, and candles. She has been a Conjure woman for over forty years and she is the fourth generation of her family to practice traditional Southern Conjure. A beloved teacher, she presents workshops across the United States. She lives in Texas, outside of Houston. Find her at *oldstyleconjure.com* or follow her on Instagram at @starrcasas.

TO OUR READERS